The Trampoline Handbook

The Ultimate Guide to Bouncing, Twisting & Flipping

by Chuck Keeney

Reviewed and Revised by Logan Christopher

DISCLAIMER

The exercises and advice contained within this book may be too strenuous or dangerous for some people, and the reader should consult with a physician before engaging in them.

The author and publisher of this book are not responsible in any manner whatsoever for any injury, which may occur through the use or misuse of the information presented here.

The Trampoline Handbook

Originally Published in 1945

Modern Reprint Edition

Manufactured in the United States of America
Published by:
Logan Christopher
Santa Cruz, California

www.lostartofhandbalancing.com

Foreword

As a kid one of my good friends had a trampoline. Almost everyday that I spent over at his house we would spend at least a little bit of time jumping and bouncing on it. We even invented a variety of games to indulge our childish imaginations. The trampoline was nothing more to us then an opportunity to have some fun.

When I grew older and got into gymnastics I began to desire to pull off tricks like handsprings, back flips and many others. My end goal was always to do these skills on the ground without any artificial aid. And for that reason I didn't use the trampoline all that much, except maybe as a way to warm-up. Unfortunately, for me I didn't realize just how useful the trampoline could be in helping me attain my goals. Doing stunts on the trampoline *does* translate to doing stunts on the floor. Even though you don't have to rely on your power to get you off the ground you still must control your body in the air. And that is a requirement for any tumbling move. Even without realizing this fact, the trampoline was still instrumental in my progression to eventually being able to doing standing backflips on the ground.

But the trampoline offers much more than an opportunity to learn tricks or just have some fun. Its also an excellent form of exercise. Rebounding on a trampoline was called by NASA in the Journal of Applied Physiology as the most effective and efficient form of exercise ever devised. Whether it's the most effective or not you can't deny that there are some unique benefits trampolining provides that other forms of training cannot.

It had been well over a year since the last time I bounced on a trampoline when serendipity struck. A woman I had just begun seeing happened to have a trampoline in her yard and shortly after that I happened across an original copy of the book you now hold in your hands. Using the book as a guide I was quickly able to master the more basic and intermediate stunts described in this book and began moving forward on the harder tricks.

Now there is no way for a single book to cover all the possible moves and combinations that can be done on the trampoline. From the easiest bounces to complicated flips with twists The Trampoline Handbook has 50 stunts described in details, with the proper moves to build up to each stunt, common errors and their corrections, plus several photos displaying the action. On top of that you have many other stunts listed that you'll be able to pull off having learned the basics that are covered in complete detail.

Now realizing the power of the trampoline, and having so much fun on it once again I knew others would benefit from the same information. Whether you bounce just for recreation or aim to compete one day this book will help you achieve your goals. Follow the instructions inside and you can't help but to make progress quickly. The best part is this book is designed for self-instruction. Though to anyone who happens to teach others how to use a trampoline, they will find this as an excellent resource and course book. In some cases spotters or safety belts are advised but they are not absolutely necessary. Depending on your skills you may be able to get by without them at all times.

I would like to thank Chuck Keeney for releasing this book in the first place many years ago, and to all of those that helped him. And now I've made it available once again for others to continue to benefit and get the most out of trampolining.

Logan Christopher

Contents

1

Getting the Most
Out of Trampolining

THE IMPORTANCE OF LEARNING

If you have ever had a chance to bounce on a trampoline, you know how much fun it can be from the very first bounce. You know, too, how much more fun it gets to be as you learn a few simple stunts, so that you no longer look and feel like a beginner. If you haven't been fortunate enough to experience this modern-day thrill, you'll just have to take our word for it and wait patiently for your first opportunity.

Along with the fun of bouncing, there are several other worthwhile benefits. Bouncing on the trampoline is the kind of strenuous exercise that most all of us need. It makes us breathe harder and deeper, as running does. It makes most of the muscles of our bodies, and especially our legs, work extra hard, get tired, and then after a good rest come back stronger than ever. It uses up calories at a good fast rate-many of us have some stored up that we can spare. If done regularly, trampolining gives us that pepped-up and alert feeling that is the result of regular vigorous exercise. The beauty of it is that while bouncing the trampoline, we can get all these benefits which accompany strenuous exercise, and all the time we're having so much fun we just don't realize that we're putting out that much energy.

Just plain carefree bouncing up and down and letting nature take its course is fun enough for a little while, but it definitely has its limitations. Unless some instruction and learning takes place, most of the possible fun in trampolining is going to be missed. With this book you can instruct yourself. It would be somewhat better to practice with one or more friends and take turns helping and teaching each other, using the instructions and pictures in this book in becoming good trampolinist and good coaches. It is best, however, to have someone with teaching experience (such as the recreation director at the playground, a physical education teacher at school, or a physical director at the "Y" or "CYO") who with their experience and the help of this book can give you a really organized course of instruction so that you can learn most quickly, thoroughly, and comfortably.

Whichever of these ways of learning works out best for you, learn you must) or you will soon lose interest, or get hurt, or both. And what's more, I've noticed during the many years I've been teaching people to do trampoline stunts that those who take the pains to learn to do each stunt really well, and try to learn the stunts in the right order, are the ones who have the most fun for the longest time. They are the ones whom everyone admires when they perform. They are the ones who have a good enough foundation so that they can, when the time is ripe, learn the more advanced, difficult, and spectacular stunts. They are the ones least likely to get hurt.

So, to have fun and continue having fun on the trampoline, keep trying to become as expert as you can. The most important trampolinist to be superior to is the trampolinist you were last week. If you continue to improve, you will continue to have fun. Improving means not only learning more stunts, but even more important, learning the stunts you know, better and better. You can improve in both ways by reading about the stunts, studying the pictures, trying the stunts, getting corrections, rereading, re-studying, and trying again and again. In this way, the great satisfactions of accomplishment can be added to the exhilaration of flying through the air with the greatest of ease, and the results in terms of fun and health will be continuous and long lasting.

BEING SAFE AND SOUND

If you learn trampoline stunts in a class on a table-high trampoline, you will be wise to follow a few simple rules for safety which the teacher will suggest. Many of the rules are those which the school or service organization must insist on to keep people from getting hurt and to protect themselves from legal liability based on negligence. If you want to make the most progress and not be slowed up by sprained joints or a wrenched back, you will cooperate fully in "going along with" the regulations. Here are a few rules which you may run into that make good sense and have sound reasons behind them.

1. Don't bounce on the trampoline while alone, and don't use the trampoline unless the teacher is supervising you or has given you permission.

2. Some of those waiting their turns should stand around the edge-especially at each end of the trampoline-and be alert and ready to give a supporting hand or push to the performer who loses his balance enough to come within reach. (On a ground-level

trampoline, such protection seems to be somewhat less effective and less necessary.)

3. Getting off a table-high trampoline can be more treacherous than it seems. When you have finished your turn, always kill your spring and then climb off. Don't leap or jump off. Don't try to step across from bed to frame. A misstep, a slippery frame, or a loose pad could give you quite a fall. (Such precautions are not as stringent for ground-level trampolines, although jumping off can be hazardous for the inexperienced and should be discouraged.)

4. In learning a new stunt or landing position, use preparatory exercises such as those suggested in this book in order to build up to the stunt gradually. It is also wise to use only as much height as is necessary to do the stunt until control is obtained; then increase the height of the bounce gradually.

5. Put the emphasis on quality rather than daring. Use a sequence of learning that establishes *sound* foundations of basic stunts before attempting the daring ones. All the stunts can be learned safely if each successive step of progress is made in a thorough-going manner. Some of them can be dangerous if attempted without sufficient background of easier stunts, *well learned*, and without taking the suggested precautions.

6. Use safety devices, when available, for learning backward somersaults and twisting somersaults. The safety belt with an overhead suspension system is most satisfactory for this purpose. Unless you have (or can get) the use of such a device or unless you are experienced in these stunts on the tumbling mat or diving board, you probably will be wise to steer clear of them. *Ability to do somersaults in the air (flips) in tumbling or diving, is not a safe basis for trying them on the trampoline without first spending many weeks or months learning the essential fundamentals of trampolining.*

7. Take short turns. If you allow yourself to become over-fatigued, you are more apt to get hurt and less likely to learn what you're trying to learn. If you have no one with whom to take turns, take frequent rest stops anyhow.

8. To have two people bouncing on the same trampoline can be more dangerous than it seems. Doubles bouncing should be done by experts only. Likewise, clowning and various forms of horseplay are deceptively treacherous and can easily lead to accidents.

If you are learning on your own trampoline in the backyard, whether it is a ground-level (pit) trampoline or a table-high model, you can be as safe or live as dangerously as you wish, depending on how completely you observe the above admonitions. Some of them may be superfluous in your particular situation, or difficult to comply with, but most of them can and should be followed by anyone bouncing on any trampoline anywhere. Each of the rules when observed will add to your safety; so when you ignore any of them, you should realize that you are doing so and be willing to accept the possible consequences.

If you are fortunate enough to live in one of the many areas where there are neighborhood trampoline centers with ground-level trampolines on which you can bounce for a modest hourly or half-hourly fee, you will be wise to observe all of their safety regulations and, in addition, the rules from the above list which they may have omitted.

For both safety and success the most important rules are those which deal with systematic step-by-step learning and with emphasis on quality. It should be a source of incentive and of reassurance to know that if the learning procedure is *sound*, the learning process will be *safe*.

2

Learning Bouncing and Landing Forms

This chapter provides much that will help you to learn plain and fancy bouncing and landing in various off-the-feet positions and returning to your feet again. Here and in the chapters that follow, are descriptions of the entire action of each of many stunts, together with sequence pictures showing various phases of their performance. There are instructions on how to proceed in learning to do the stunts and on how to correct the mistakes you may find yourself making.

To use all this material to best advantage, it is suggested that you read the description and study the pictures to get a mental picture of yourself going through the correct motions. Second, read the learning procedure, going through each step mentally. Now, if you have a trampoline handy, try each step in succession, practicing each a number of times until the entire stunt can be accomplished. From time to time refer back to the book for corrections of form and of other errors, and continue to practice, trying always to improve. Working together with others for mutual help and correction will be most beneficial. Start learning the next stunt when you begin to get bored practicing the old ones. It is certainly neither necessary nor advisable to stay with one stunt until you have perfected it before going on to another. Be sure, however, to review the old stunts often in order to continue to improve them.

Keep in mind that throughout the book the photographs and the descriptions are meant to complement each other. Neither one is as helpful alone as both are together. Sometimes in studying the pictures you will discover something about a stunt not mentioned in the description. The pictures may remind you of some point of good form (by its presence or by its conspicuous absence in the picture) which for brevity may not be mentioned in the description of that phase of the stunt. It is even more true that the pictures alone will not give you all the information you need to know. Obviously it is impractical to show every segment of every stunt in pictures. I have tried to show the parts of each stunt which make it different from others and, at the same time, to give an effect of sequence for each set of pictures. Reading the descriptions will help you to clarify the picture sequences.

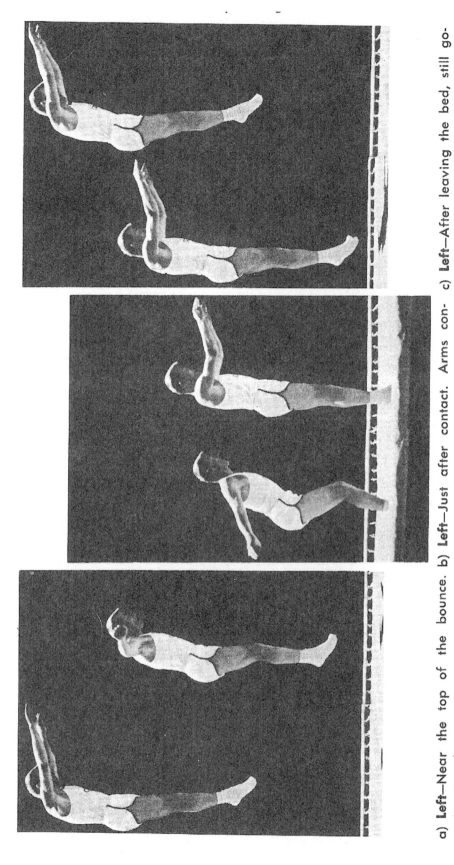

a) **Left**—Near the top of the bounce. Starting down.
Right—Nearing the bed on the descent. Arms start circle.

b) **Left**—Just after contact. Arms continue circular sweep.
Right—After sinking deep into the bed, on the way up again.

c) **Left**—After leaving the bed, still going up.
Right—Reaching the peak again.

Fig. 1. Controlled bounces.

Stunt NO.1—CONTROllED BOUNCES

DESCRIPTION OF ACTION. During the feet-to-feet bounce and during most other stunts (unless otherwise indicated), your direction of vision should be forward and downward. You should be looking at a point on the bed itself which is about five feet forward of your landing and take-off spot. Looking forward at approximately this distance, you should be able to see peripherally your feet and also some of the surroundings. This direction of vision is much better than looking too straight down, which tends to tip you forward, or too straight, ahead, which gives you less accurate information about your landing place and your timing.

During the bounce, your feet and legs, should be together, straight, and pointed most of the time. On the landing, however, (as on all landings on the feet) they should spread from 12 'to 18 inches apart and lose their point as the whole sole of the foot comes into contact with the bed. The knees bend a little for a short time just before and during this contact period and then straighten again as the bottom of the depression of the bed is reached (Fig. 1b). As your legs straighten, your foot muscles drive also, and the feet return to a pointed position as they leave the bed. The legs come together again on the upward flight and this position is held until time to prepare for the next contact.

Your arm action during the bouncing is very important for appearance, balance and, most of all, for adding downward force to the landing, which in turn increases the lift you get from the trampoline. During the upward flight, the arms swing forward and upward, shoulder-width apart, until they are in the area forward of and above the head (Fig. 1c). Here they stop, waiting for just the right instant during the downward flight to start their forceful, circular sweep. This sweep starts by spreading the arms and continues by circling them backward and downward without bending them (Fig. 1a). The lower part of this sweep corresponds to the contact period of the bounce (while feet are on the bed) and adds to the downward force into the bed (see Fig. 1b). The emphasis of the arm swing should be on the downward force, not on the lift up afterward.

STEPS IN LEARNING

1. Before you get on the trampoline, try straightening your knee and pointing your foot. Now sit down and try it with both legs and both feet, holding them together and tight.

2. Try jumping up from the floor, straightening and pointing the legs while in the air. Unpoint before landing again. Repeat this exercise many times.

3. Now, on the trampoline, try a series of *small* bounces without arm action but with emphasis on leg form. Don't try to pull the legs together while in the air as yet; just leave them about 12 inches apart all the way.

4. Back on the floor, now, try the arm action along with the leg action as you take a series of jumps off the floor. (You can still leave the legs apart for this exercise.)

5. Now see if you can do the bounce series on the trampoline, using the correct head and eyes position and arm and leg actions and positions.

6. As you get more practice, learn to bring your legs together after the feet leave the bed, before the top of the bounce, and spread them on the way down before landing again. You should also get more force and height

as soon as you can do so without losing control. Perfecting this bounce is so important because it is part of almost every other stunt. You have to get bouncing with proper height and control before you can do any of the many other stunts successfully.

CORRECTION OF ERRORS

A. Arching the body at the top of the bounce makes the control less good. Try, instead, to bend forward a very little at that point so that your feet are visible in the lower part of your field of vision.

B. Drawing the knees up during the descent and then driving the feet toward the bed does not increase height. This action results in pounding the bed which spoils timing. Correct timing and forceful arm action are the primary means of increasing height.

Stunt No. 2-KNEE-BREAK STOP

DESCRIPTION OF ACTION. The knee-break stop is a simple thing to accomplish and one that you should learn very early in your bouncing experience. It is a means of stopping your bounce immediately and gracefully. It should be used at the end of a series of bounces, at the end of any stunt unless a rebound is desired, and whenever the bounces or stunts are getting out of control.

The descent toward the bed is made in the same manner as usual, but instead of the slight knee bend followed by a quick knee straightening during the contact period which gives you the rebound, let your knees bend more and stay bent so that the

rebound force is absorbed in the knees and the feet do not leave the bed (Fig. 2). This is not a deep squat landing, only a medium knee bend after the feet contact the bed to absorb the rebound force.

Fig. 2. Knee-break stop. The bend-ing of the knees has killed the rebound.

Stunt NO.3-VARIETY BOUNCES (Swan, Tuck, Jackknife, Open Pike, Closed Pike, and Straddle Pike)

DESCRIPTION OF ACTION. These are six somewhat different and yet somewhat similar stunts. Swan, tuck, and pike are the names of the three fundamental body positions used both in springboard diving, and in trampolining. The pike has three different common alternate positions: jackknife, open pike, and closed pike; and one uncommon or freak position: the straddle pike. For the present, you are to put your body into one of these positions (instead of the normal slightly bent position recommended for the controlled bounces) during the highest part of the flight of a feet-to-feet bounce. No rotation is involved; you just keep the vertical balance while changing into the intended position briefly and back again into the feet-landing position.

The swan bounce (Fig. 3a) is done by swinging your arms forward and upward and spreading them until they reach a position a little above shoulder level and in line with, or somewhat behind, the shoulders. This arm swing is done as you leave the bed on an upward flight while bouncing and is accompanied by a slight arching of the body (hyperextension). The position is held briefly at the peak of the jump and part way down, then is released so that you can make a proper landing and arm swing for a rebound. These jumps can be done singly, mixed with straight bounces, consecutively one right after another, or alternating with tuck or pike bounces.

To do a tuck bounce (Fig. 3b), you go into a doubled-up, bent-at-the-waist, bent-at-the-knees position before you reach the top of the lift but after you have taken the complete leg drive. In the tuck position, the hands are usually cupped across the middle of the shin with the arms pulling in to tighten the position. As with the swan bounce, this position is released and the regular jumping position resumed in time to make a good landing and rebound.

The pike bounces are similar, except that the high-in-the-air positions are those in which the body is bent sharply at the waist, but the knees are kept straight. The hands reach downward to touch the front of the pointed feet at the top of the bounce in the jackknife bounce (Fig. 3c). The arms open to a swan position with the body bent to attain the position for the open pike bounce (Fig. 3d). The hands are cupped under the knee and the arms are bent to bring the face close to the straight knees in the closed pike bounce (Fig. 3e). The legs are spread wide and the hands reach to the pointed feet in the straddle pike bounce (Fig. 3f).

In all these forms the feet should remain pointed and the direction of vision should remain forward and downward, as in the controlled bounce to aid balance and timing.

a) Swan bounce.   b) Tuck bounce.   c) Jackknife bounce.

Fig. 3. Variety bounces.

STEPS IN LEARNING

1. The controlled bounces and the knee-break stop should be fairly well learned before trying these variety bounces.

2. The air position of the swan, tuck, or pike, should be practiced in a lying, sitting, or standing position on the floor before trying it in mid-air.

3. Trying these air positions from a standing jump from the floor will help to give you the necessary feel of the balance involved and will make you appreciate the nice lift the trampoline gives you.

4. First attempts of the whole stunt on the trampoline should be low and conservative until balance is acquired. Height should be added when it can be done without losing control. Height, balance, and precise form are the elements that make these positions fun to do and attractive to watch.

CORRECTION OF ERRORS

A. If there is a tendency to come down in an off-balance forward lean after opening from a tuck or pike position, it is probably due to trying to reach down to touch the toes or grasp the legs rather than lifting the legs up to meet the hands or arms halfway. To correct, wait until you are near the height of your bounce, and then move the trunk and legs closer together by both lifting the legs and bending forward from the waist.

B. If you are landing tipped forward after the swan bounce, you need to emphasize the pull-back of the shoulders and underemphasize the throw-back of the legs in attaining the body arch. If you are tipping backward, the opposite correction is in order.

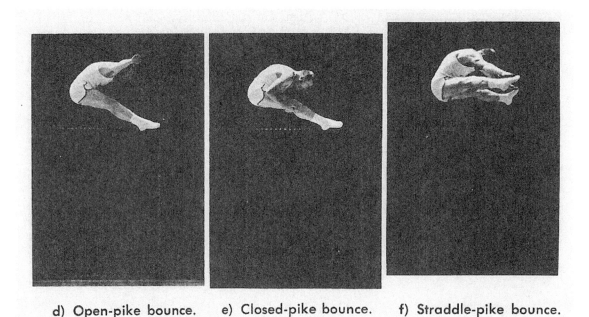

d) Open-pike bounce.   e) Closed-pike bounce.   f) Straddle-pike bounce.

Fig. 3. Continued.

C. If you are losing height on the next bounce after one of these positions, it may be that you are not getting your arms in position to take a regular circular arm beat. After you release your position and are descending, you should be preparing your arms for the down beat that increases the force of your next lift.

Stunt No.4—SIT DROP

DESCRIPTION OF ACTION. After a few preliminary bounces, you leave the bed as if going into another bounce except that you push the hips more forward and pull the shoulders more backward (Fig. 4a). In this way you tip your slightly arched body backward. You do not jump backward or travel backward, but simply tip backward. Your arms, following their usual forward and upward swing, stop well above shoulder level, pause, and then start circling back to their landing position. Your legs, of course, remain together, straight, and pointed; and your eyes are looking forward and downward (Fig. 4b).

Just when your feet are about to touch the mat on the downward trip, you should bend at the waist just enough so that the whole backside of each leg hits the bed at the same time. As you land, your trunk should be leaning backward a little from the waist and your hands should be on the bed a foot or so behind your hips and six inches or so wider than your hips. Your hands should be placed with fingers pointing forward toward your feet and your arms should be slightly bent (Fig. 4c).

The bed of course goes down as you contact it and comes back up lifting you with it. As you feel the lift, you should start a mild forward swing of the trunk and an arm-straightening push with the hands.

As you get lifted up off the bed, straighten out again at the waist (without bending the knees), ready for a stand-up landing. Your arms should swing forward during this recovery to the feet so that they can be in a forward-upward position for balance on the landing or for an arm beat on the rebound.

STEPS IN LEARNING

1. You should have learned the controlled bounces and knee-break stop fairly well, but need not have worked on Stunt NO.3 before learning the sit drop.

2. On the trampoline or on the floor, place yourself in the sit landing position, as described above. Check each detail of correct form. Now practice the mild forward trunk swing and arm straightening.

3. In a standing position practice the mild forward hip thrust and backward shoulder pull which, when done later on a bounce, will give you the backward tilt.

4. Now on the trampoline, from a small bounce try the backward-tilted straight-body drop, change to the sit position, and recover to the feet. Do this many times until you are doing it right most of the time.

5. Little by little, increase the force of the bounce until you attain full height without losing your form and control.

6. After learning a sit drop or any stunt as an isolated single stunt, it is well to learn to "swing out of it." This means that you finish it in such a manner that you have the balance and force to make the last landing of the stunt serve at the same time as the take-off into another

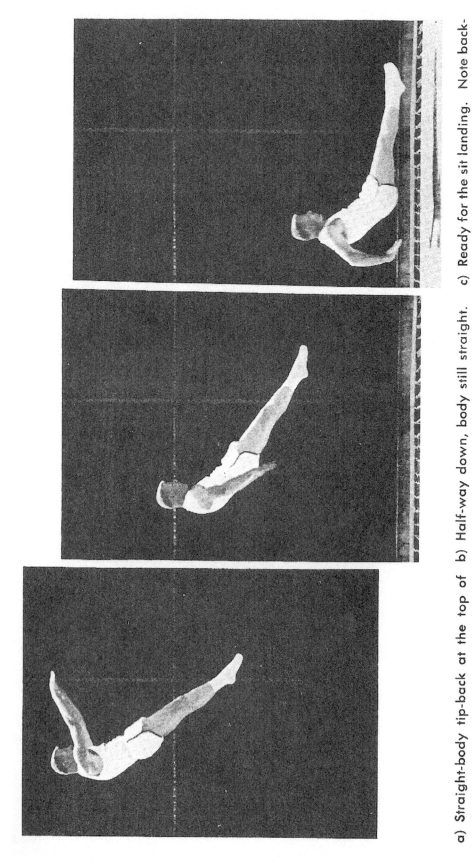

a) Straight-body tip-back at the top of the bounce.

b) Half-way down, body still straight.

c) Ready for the sit landing. Note backward lean. After the sit will come the forward lean and rebound to standing.

Fig. 4. Sit drop.

stunt of the same or different variety. If this is your intention, it is well to learn to get the arms forward and upward above head level (as at the top of the straight bounce) during the interval between leaving the sitting position (or other position in other stunts) and landing on the feet again. This arm preparation will permit you to use the swinging force of your arms with their strong downward circular sweep to help you push the bed down and thereby get a bigger lift for your next stunt.

CORRECTION OF ERRORS

A. Landing heels first instead of on the whole backside of the legs and landing bent forward at the waist are usually results of not enough backward tip of the body axis. More hip thrust and shoulder pull are indicated to correct these errors.

B. Having the bent-at-the-waist, sitting-in-the-air position during the flight is a permissible, but inferior form. It can be avoided by pushing your midsection forward early and keeping your body straight until the last moment.

C. After the sit drop, landing on the feet in an off-balance forward position is probably due to too strong a forward swing of the trunk and too forceful an arm push during the lift after the sit landing. Only a little of these are needed to get you up to a stand. More will be needed in subsequent stunts such as sit drop to front drop, swivel hips; etc.

Stunt No. 5—HANDS-AND-KNEES DROP

DESCRIPTION OF ACTION. From a rebounding take-off you tip forward slightly as you leave the bed in a form otherwise the same as in the straight bounce. At the top of the bounce you bend forward at the waist, bend the knees to a right angle, and reach the arms downward toward the bed, keeping them about shoulder width apart (Fig. 5a).

The back, from shoulders to hips, should be about level and parallel with the bed as you descend toward the bed (Fig. 5b). The landing is made on the hands-and-knees with arms slightly bent but firm and with knees about six inches apart (Fig. 5c).

After you sink into the bed in this position and are about to be lifted up, you can assist by straightening your arms and pushing with your hands. This push and the lift of the bed, along with the straightening of your waist and knees, will bring you up again to a standing position.

STEPS IN LEARNING

1. You should have some proficiency in the controlled bounces and the knee-break stop before you learn the hands-and-knees drop, but you need not have even tried Stunts Nos. 3 and 4.

2. On the floor, get down into the landing position. Bend your arms just enough to put your back level. Your knees should be right under your hips. Your hands should be right under your shoulders. Practice the arm push a few times.

3. On the trampoline, take a series of low bounces without arm swing and on one of these, tip forward and bend into the landing position, land, push, and return to feet. Do lots of these.

4. Now, with a bigger bounce and arm swing, try the whole stunt. Keep practicing until you are consistently landing with your back level and

a) Forward tip and forward bend on the way up.

b) Semi-tuck on the way down.

c) Ready for the hands-and-knees landing. The bounce from hands-and-knees to feet will follow.

Fig. 5.   Hands-and-knees drop.

with your hands and knees hitting the bed at the same time.

5. Learn to "swing out" of these landings into consecutive hands-and-knees drops and other stunts.

CORRECTION OF ERRORS

A. If you are landing with your hands before your knees instead of at the same time, you should not bend forward at the waist quite so soon.

B. If you are landing on your knees before your hands, or landing in a sitting-on-your-haunches position instead of with knees under hips, you should probably bend forward at the waist a little more or a little sooner.

C. If you are landing level, but are unable to bounce back to your feet or can do so only with difficulty, you need to utilize the bent arm landing followed by an arm-straightening push.

Stunt NO.6-KNEE DROP

DESCRIPTION OF ACTION. You should use a bouncing take-off identical to that for the controlled bounces. At the top of the bounce or on the way down, you bend the knee joints to right angle positions (Fig. 6a). You keep the knees bent as you land. The circular arm sweep (beat) is the same as on the controlled bounce, but is delayed slightly because of the slightly later landing on the knees instead of feet. It is important not to bend at the waist more than a very little bit and even more important not to arch at the waist (hips forward) as this may result in a wrenched back (Fig. 6b). As you are being lifted by the bed, your arms continue their upward swing and you begin to straighten out your knees ready for your stand-up landing (Fig. 6c).

STEPS IN LEARNING

1. This stunt may be learned right after Stunts Nos. land 2, without learning Nos. 3, 4, or 5 first.

2. On the floor, kneel in an erect position with your hips straight (not arched) and your toes pointed back (not down). Practice the arm circling beat while in this position.

3. On the trampoline, from a small bounce, drop to your knees and return to your feet.

4. Add the arm swing and additional height to Step 3.

5. Learn to swing out of your landing into another stunt of the same or a different variety. Use your arm circle beat on your feet landing between stunts.

CORRECTION OF ERRORS

A. If you have difficulty landing in good balance and returning to your feet under control, you need more practice on the controlled bounce, and you need to remember not to change your vertical balance while bending your knees for the drop.

B. If you are feeling any strain in the back from this, you are trying to keep too straight and consequently getting the hips out of line forward; i.e., arching (hyperextending) the back on landing on your

a) Before the knee landing. Arms poised ready for the "beat." b) Just after contact. Arm swing has started. c) Coming back to a stand-up on the rebound. Arms still swinging upward.

Fig. 6. Knee drop.

knees. It would be better to be a very little bit bent at the waist to avoid this error.

Stunt No. 7—STRAIGHT-KNEE BACK DROP

DESCRIPTION OF ACTION. From a rebounding take-off, you immediately pull your shoulders back a little and at the same time bend sharply at the waist, thereby tipping the body axis backward. It is well also to be traveling backward. Your legs remain straight, together, and pointed, and your head retains its looking-forward-and-downward position so that as you rotate backwards your chin comes closer to your chest (Fig. 7a). Your hands may come onto the front part of the leg just above the knee as in the illustration or may be kept free alongside and not touching the legs.

In this position, then, you make your landing, contacting the bed with the entire back from the shoulder blades to the base of the spine (Fig. 7b). Your head should not touch the bed but should stay forward with chin on chest as you sink into the bed and are lifted again into the air. The area of this landing should be two to four feet behind the line from which the feet departed.

To bounce back to your feet from this on-the-back landing, you should start unbending (opening) at the waist as you are lifted by the bed, straightening out completely before landing on the feet again (Fig. 7c). A push against your legs with your hands will be helpful in starting this opening action. The legs remain straight and the feet pointed throughout the entire action until just before the final landing on the feet.

STEPS IN LEARNING

1. Considerable background of experience and practice should precede the learning of the back drop. Stunts Nos. 1, 2, and 4 should certainly come before this one and some pike bounces (see Stunt No. 3) also would be helpful. It is recommended that all six previously described stunts be learned before the back drop.

2. On the floor, lie on your back with your legs straight up (a right angle bend at your waist) as in the landing position of the back drop. In slow motion, go through the opening-at-the-waist movement finishing flat on the back.

3. Go through Step 2, lying on the trampoline instead of the floor, making the opening movement faster though by no means as fast as possible. The final position, as in Step 2, is to be flat on the back.

4. Stand on the trampoline. Try dropping to the back landing position by lifting one leg up in front, jumping slightly from the other, and then joining the legs before coming to the bed. As you are being lifted up again, open fairly vigorously to regain the straight position standing.

5. From a series of low bounces, take off from both feet, tip back, lift both legs and do the back drop, as previously described.

6. Increasing height should be cautiously added on successive attempt only as you can do so without losing control. An overturn onto the back of the neck from a medium or high bounce can be both uncomfortable and dangerous.

7. Learn to swing out of these back drops into other easier stunts

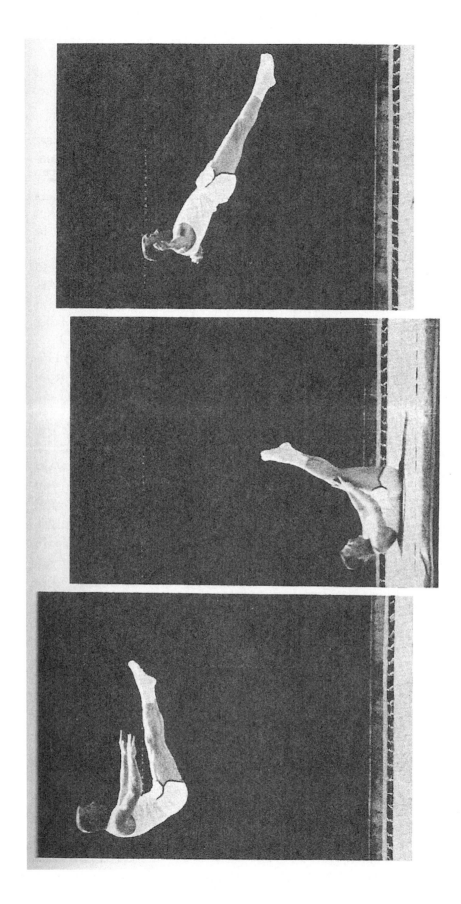

a) Dropping toward the back landing b) The landing on the back position. c) Body straightens out for rebound to a with body bent and knees straight. Knees could be straighter. stand.

Fig. 7. Straight-knee back drop.

first, and later you can learn to do several consecutive back drops in swing time.

CORRECTION OF ERRORS

A. Trying to sit up while returning from the back landing to the feet results in an inferior lift and a bent-over landing. Simply straightening the body at the waist, making no attempt to swing the upper body forward, will result in the right kind of rebound to the feet. You must open up from the piked landing on the back to the straight position as if you were trying to make the next landing fiat on the back as in Step 3 above.

B. Letting the knees bend at the moment of contact on the back and while sinking into the bed kills the force of the rebound and makes returning to the feet more difficult. It is well to learn this stunt with the knees straight throughout. Another type of back drop utilizing bent legs during part of the action will be described in Stunt No. 9.

C. Difficulty in coming back up to the feet can sometimes be traced to failure to move backward during the drop. The hips should land from 2 to 4 feet behind the point of take-off.

Stunt No.8-FRONT DROP

DESCRIPTION OF ACTION. As you go into the air for the bounce on which you intend to make a front landing, you bend forward at the waist very slightly at first (Fig. 8a). As you reach the top of the bounce, you increase the bend at the waist enough to bring your body into a horizontal position over the bed as it descends to a few feet above the bed (Fig. 8b). Just before your feet and hands come to the bed, you must open up again at the waist and make your landing in the proper position (Fig. 8c). After sinking into the bed, you add to the lift the trampoline will give you by pushing with the hands. The return to a stand-up landing is completed by bending again a little at the waist with and after your push. If you are going to swing out of this landing into another front drop or some other stunt, you will need to remember to lift your arms to the forward-upward position during the interval between pushing off the bed with them and landing on the feet so that as you land you can circle-sweep them down to get a better lift into your next stunt.

The proper landing position on the front is of great importance to you for comfort, safety, and a forceful rebound. The landing should be flat with your entire front side from chest to knees making contact with the bed at the same time. The arms are extended forward, bent at the elbow with the palms facing downward. The forearms and the hands make a strong resisting contact against the bed at the same time as the body lands. The hands are close together (about 2 or 3 inches apart and at a point on the bed just beyond the top of the head. The bent elbows are wide apart and on the bed at points about opposite the performer's ears. The knees are allowed to bend as the landing is made.

STEPS IN LEARNING

1. The controlled bounces and knee-break stop (Stunts Nos. 1 and 2), and the hands-and-knees drop (Stunt No.5) are essential prerequisites to learning the front drop. A good start at learning the remainder of the first seven stunts would be advisable before undertaking the front drop.

a) On the way up. Hips moving backward, shoulders moving forward. b) On the way down. Body bent to semi-jackknife. c) Just before landing. Body still a little bent. Forearms reaching for contact. Bouncing up to the feet will follow.

Fig. 8. Front drop.

2. On the floor, put yourself in the front-landing position as described above. Hug the floor with both the chest and the upper legs. Check to see if the position of your arms is correct. The chin should be just above the floor. The feet do not touch the floor. As a contrast to this, try an arched-back lying position with knees and chest off the floor and only the midsection on the floor. This arched position is a wrong position and one to be avoided. Return to the correct flat position and get the "feel" of it again.

3. On the trampoline, get on your hands-and-knees. With a little trial-and-error practice you can learn to bounce up and down (small bounces) on your hands-and-knees without bucking. When you can do so, practice bouncing from the hands-and-knees position to the front landing and return to hands-and-knees. On this exercise, the higher you bounce the longer you hold the hands-and-knees landing position after you leave the bed before you straighten out to make the front landing. Do this exercise many times until the correct landing position becomes a habit.

4. Next, try a hands-and-knees landing from a standing-up bounce, and instead of returning immediately to the feet, as in the hands-and-knees drop, go instead from the hands-and-knees landing to a front landing, back to hands-and-knees landing, and then return to the stand. After a few of these, you can eliminate the second hands-and-knees landing, returning to the feet directly from the front landing.

5. Practice, now, a few hands-and-knees drops with a somewhat abnormal form. On these particular drops, double up a little more than normal, both at the knees and at the waist while in the air, before the hands-and-knees landing and get into this semi-tucked position earlier in your flight than you would for an ordinary hands-and-knees drop. Practice these until you are consistently landing level; i.e., with the back horizontal and with the knees and hands (with slightly bent arms) landing all at the same time.

6. Go into the air as if you were going to do one of the hands-and-knees drops as in Step 5, but just before you land on hands and knees, open instead to the front landing. Come from the front landing up to a stand. Do these low at first. The higher you bounce, the later you should bend forward and double up.

7. After learning the semi-tucked front drop in Step 5, you will want to learn the semi-jackknife form as in the illustration. To learn to substitute the straight-knee, bent-at-the-waist position for the doubled-up, knees-bent position in the air, it will be helpful to go back through Steps 3, 4, and 5, using a kind of pyramid position landing (hands and feet on bed, knees straight, hands about 24 inches forward of the feet) in place of the hands-and-knees landings, and the semi-jackknife in place of the semi-tuck in mid-air. This will prepare you for the complete stunt which is the same as Step 6, but with the semi-jackknife form.

CORRECTION OF ERRORS

A. Getting your body into a straight position early in the flight and then dropping in this position to the bed is an error in technique. It is much more difficult to be consistent with this inferior form. Consistency is important in front drops to avoid back strains. Use the semi-tuck or semi-pike position for the in-the-air position, flattening at the last instant onto the bed.

B. Overturning to an unlevel, chest-first landing, is usually the result of making the forward bend at the waist too early. It could be the result of too complete a bend or of holding the bend too long.

C. Underturning to an unlevel, knees-first landing is a result of bending too late, too little, or too briefly.

D. To avoid a forward movement in the drop, resulting in a skidding, forward-moving landing, the hips must be moved backward as the shoulders move forward into the bend, thereby keeping the center of the weight over the point of take-off.

E. Inability to recover easily to the feet after the front landing can often be cured by using a backward-sliding, continuous, downward pressure with the hands against the bed while coming up from the front landing.

Stunt No. 9—KICK-OUT BACK DROP

DESCRIPTION OF ACTION. This variety of back drop is similar of course to the straight-knee back drop (Stunt No.7), but is sufficiently different and so important in its uses that we feel justified in treating it as a separate stunt.

As you take off on one of your bounces, you tip back slightly; and as soon as your legs have completed their good knee-straightening drive, you double up your legs into a tight tuck position (Fig. 9a). This position with the knees and hips flexed as far as possible, the chin on the chest, and the arms alongside the legs but not grasping or touching them, is held until you make contact with your back on the bed a few inches behind your starting place. The action at this instant is a leg-straightening kick-out in an upward direction (Fig. 9b). This kick-out action includes some straightening at the waist as well as at the knees. The timing of the kick-out is very important. It should be completed during the interval between the first contact and the beginning of the return lift as the deepest position in the bed is reached. The return to the feet can be made either in the style shown in the straight-knee back drop (Stunt No.7) by kicking out at about a 45-degree angle and straightening the body, or in the style shown in the kick-out back drop illustration (Fig. 9c). In this second or sit-up style, the point of aim on the kick-out is only a little forward of straight up. The kick is followed by a sit-up action and then, at the top, the legs are dropped out of the pike (sitting) position into a regular stand-up landing.

STEPS IN LEARNING

1. Before you try to learn this one, you should certainly be able to do controlled bounces, tuck bounces, sit drops, and straight-knee back drops. It would be well also if you have made some progress at learning most or all of the other stunts that precede this one.

2. Using a small bounce, try the tuck bounce, as described in Stunt No. 3, but without grasping your legs with your hands. Do a few of these until they become easy.

3. Jump into the doubled-up position again, and this time tip backwards slightly, hold the tuck all the way down, landing with the hands on the bed alongside and behind the hips in a tucked sit landing. Return to a stand on the rebound as in the ordinary sit drop.

4. After Step 3 has been successfully practiced a number of times, you can begin to add a little more backward tip and try for a tucked back

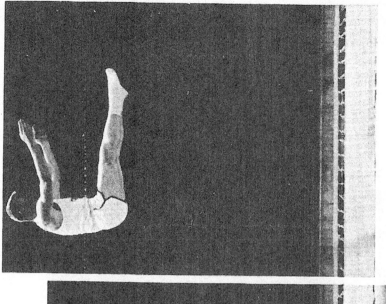

a) Tucked up early. Dropping toward the bed.

b) After going down into the bed and being lifted up again. The kick-out is almost complete before leaving the bed.

c) This sit-up in the air will be followed by a body-straightening drop to a standing position to finish the stunt.

Fig. 9. Kick-out back drop.

drop landing, eliminating of course the hand support used in the sit landing. This should be done quite low at first and without trying to rebound to the feet. It is important in this exercise to keep the chin tight against the chest, especially on landing. Overturning onto the back of the neck should be carefully avoided. It pays to be overcautious until you find out by experimenting just how little tip it takes in this tuck position to get onto the back.

5. When you can consistently land in the right position on your back, you can add the kick-out to complete the stunt. It is helpful to remember that this kick-out, if done at the right time, will serve to push you deeper into the bed, so that the springs will give you a bigger lift. It is not an attempt to kick yourself up after you have gone all the way down and have started up again.

CORRECTION OF ERRORS

A. Putting the hands on the shins during the drop to the back will usually result in getting too late a kick-out. Keep the hands free.

B. Letting the knees bend more after contact with the back on the bed has been made will kill the rebound. Have them bent early and completely so that they can start kicking out early enough.

C. If your kick is too late, it gives you little or no lift and makes it difficult to come to your feet. Time the kick with the first contact.

D. Kicking out at too low an angle will result in overturning the final landing or in coming up to a stand too soon without a good arc. To aim higher on the kick-out, it is necessary to have the knees in close to the chest on the back landing. It may also be helpful to use a toes-turned-up form instead of pointed feet just before the kick-out.

E. Overturning the back drop landing can result in a strained neck or an inferior rebound or both. This error is a result of tipping back as much for the kick-out back drop as you would in a straight-knee back drop, thus failing to allow for the greater ease of rotation in the tucked position. Review the steps suggested in the learning procedure to correct this fault.

Stunt No. 10—BACK PULLOVER

DESCRIPTION OF ACTION. The preliminary bounces before the back pullover should bring you a bit forward of the center of the trampoline so that you will have adequate room behind you. The take-off and drop for this stunt are very much like those for the straight-knee back drop (Stunt No. 7). The three differences are that on this stunt you do not travel backward on the drop, but try to land about where you take off: you grasp the legs under the knees instead of putting the hands on the front of the legs; and you land about half-way between sitting and on the back, instead of square on the back (Fig. 10a). During the drop you keep a little bit open at the waist; but just as you hit on the point of your V position, you pull with your arms, closing the body jackknife tighter and aiding the backward rolling motion (Fig. 10b). During this drop, landing, and pull, the head is kept tucked down, chin-to-chest. As the trampoline bed lifts you up, you continue to rotate backward and continue to pull against the back of your legs until your feet are in a position to come down to the bed (Fig. 10c). During this time you straighten out, raise your head, and finally come to a stand-up landing.

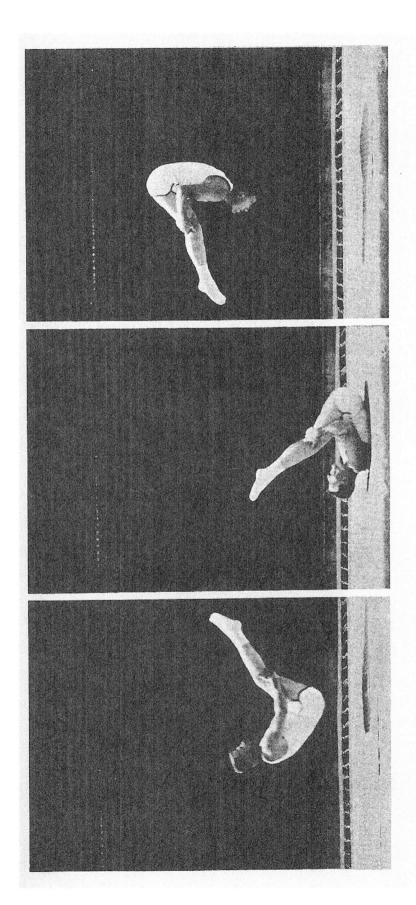

a) Dropping toward the point-of-the-V landing.

b) After going down into the bed and being lifted up. The tight pull-in has rotated the body backward.

c) After leaving the bed, the backward rotation continues toward a stand-up landing.

Fig. 10. Back pullover.

STEPS IN LEARNING

1. Before undertaking to learn the back pullover, you should certainly be able to do controlled bounces, sit drops, pike bounces, hands-and-knees drops, and straight-knee back drops.

2. To get the feel of the pull-in and the backward rotation, take a sort of sitting position on the trampoline bed, balanced on the hips, with the hands grasped under the knees and with the legs and feet up forward off the bed. Now suddenly increase the bend at your waist by pulling with your arms. This will roll you onto the back of your neck, at which point you stop, return to your original position, and then repeat the exercise several more times.

3. From a small bounce, try the drop action without doing any pull-in and consequently no backward-rolling action. Just try to land between a sit landing and a straight-knee back drop landing with the legs at a little more than a 45-degree angle above the bed on one side and the trunk at a little less than a 45-degree angle above the bed on the other side of the point of contact.

4. When you can consistently hit at the correct angle, then, still using the low bounce, try to combine the pull-in of Step 2 with the drop of Step 3 by pulling just as contact with the bed is first made. The rebound and the pull-in should lift you up and turn you over backward and allow you to land at least as far over as on your hands and knees. A little more height on the preliminary bounce with the same technique will make it possible for you to land on your feet.

CORRECTION OF ERRORS

A. Letting the knees bend a little as you pull in with your arms is necessary for most individuals. Considerable knee bend is a useful technique to increase the rotation when trying to make a landing beyond the feet such as a sit drop, another back pullover or a back drop.

B. Failure to get enough backward rotation to come easily to a stand is due either to a poorly timed or weak pull-in or to a failure to hit the right position on the drop. Either landing in too much of a sit position or landing in too much of a back drop position will make the backward rotation slower and more difficult. Try a V balance on the floor to get fixed in your mind and muscles the right position for the landing.

C. Getting too much backward rotation can be corrected either by pulling in a little less hard or by opening up sooner after pulling.

3

Easy Combinations
and Twists

The fundamental bounces and landings have been pictured and described in Chapter 2. I wish to remind you again of the importance of learning to do them well if you expect to go ahead and learn to perform the new stunts in this chapter easily and safely. Of the eight stunts presented in this chapter, four of them (Nos. 12, 13, 15, and 16) are combination stunts which involve bouncing from one fundamental landing to another without coming to your feet in between. The other four (Nos. 11, 14, 17, and 18) are examples of fundamental landings either preceded by or followed by half twists. A half twist is a turn of 180 degrees which leaves you facing in the opposite direction from your original or previous position. To learn these stunts most easily, you should follow the suggestions made in the first paragraph of Chapter 2. After you have learned these eight stunts, many similar, equally easy combinations and twists will come to mind. Many of them you will be able to learn by trial-and-error methods based on the skills and understanding which you will have acquired by that time. At the end of the present chapter, you will find a list of some of these additional stunts, a few of which you may not have thought of previously.

Stunt No. 11—HALF TWIST TO SIT DROP

DESCRIPTION OF ACTION. The take-off bounce for this stunt is done with a moderate forward tip and usually with a little forward travel. As your take-off lift progresses, your arms are swung overhead with a turn of the shoulders to the right or to the left. With your legs and body held straight, the trunk, hips, and legs follow the twist started by the shoulders (Fig. 11a). Approximately 90 degrees of the right or left twist of the body is accomplished by the time the greatest height is reached. Your head, however, should maintain its forward position as much as possible, continuing to look in the original direction during this entire twisting lift and through part of the descent. As your body continues its flight, it also continues its twist (Fig. 11 b). About halfway through the downward part of the flight lower your arms, turn your head around to its final position, and bend at the waist to a backward-leaning sit landing (Fig. 11c). This landing puts you in excellent position to rebound to the feet or to some other desired position.

STEPS IN LEARNING

1. Good controlled bounces and sit drops are the only essential prerequisites to this stunt, but considerable experience with other stunts is recommended.

2. Stand on the trampoline with your arms reaching overhead. Rise onto your tiptoes and start falling forward (like a tree after it has been chopped through). As you fall, gradually turn your shoulders and body, but not your head. When about halfway down on your fall, lower your hands, turn your head and complete your twist. Make a sit landing facing the opposite direction from your starting position. You need not try to rebound to your feet on this exercise. That can be added when you are starting from a bounce instead of from a stand. The twist should be smooth, except for your head which turns around all at once.

3. After several successful attempts at Step 2 try the same thing, starting from a small bounce with the arms reaching overhead while bouncing. You will need to tip forward and travel forward on the bounce on which you intend to twist. This time you can bounce up to your feet after the sit landing. You should practice this until it is smooth and sure.

4. Now it should be easy to use your regular arm-circling action on your preliminary bounces, carrying the arms upward to overhead on the final take-off into the shoulder-turned, delayed-head, stretching twist to sit landing. Keep the height moderate at first and then on later attempts see how high you can take it, without sacrificing smoothness and form.

CORRECTION OF ERRORS

A. Landing in an erect or forward-leaning sit position after the twist is an error which can be traced to insufficient forward tip during the take-off action.

B. Landing on the seat with the feet up in the air is usually a result of bending too much and, often, too soon at the waist.

C. Too early a head turn, bent body while twisting, lack of overhead reach, and failure to keep the legs straight, together, and pointed are all errors which are important to watch for and correct if you want to have the best looking style-one which you can "work out of" and one that later will help you to learn

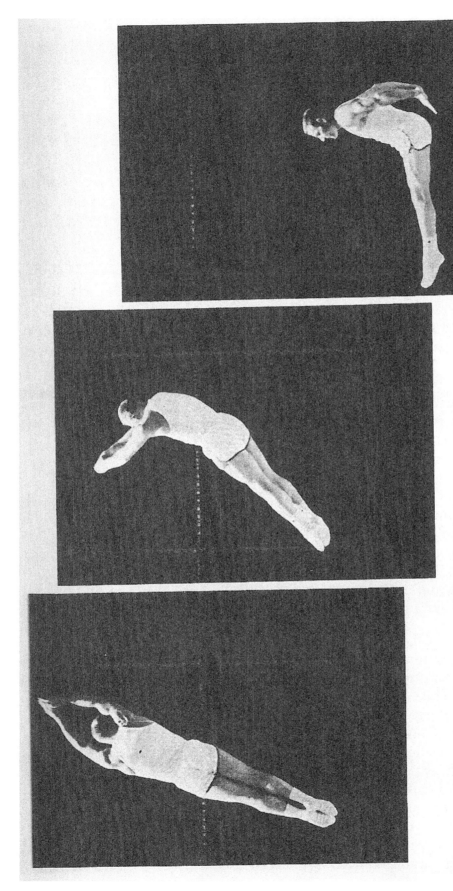

a) At the top of the bounce. Twist partly accomplished; head not yet turned.

b) On the way down. Head has turned; twist almost complete; body bending.

c) All ready for the sit landing. Bounce to feet will follow.

Fig. 11. Half twist to sit drop.

related stunts.

Stunt No. 12—SIT DROP TO FRONT DROP

DESCRIPTION OF ACTION. The take-off, the tip-back, and the body positions are the same at the beginning of this stunt as they are for the sit drop (Stunt No.4). The different action begins just after your sit landing while the bed is lowering and then lifting. During this interval your upper body should swing forward more vigorously, from the backward-leaning position, thus giving you more forward rotation (Fig. 12a). During this fairly low flight from the sit to the front landing, your body and knees may be flexed in a semi-tuck position. The preferred form, however, is to keep the knees straight making this a pike position (Fig. 12b). With either form the bend is held until you can open out to a flat front landing (Fig. 12c). From the front, the recovery to the feet is as described for the front drop (Stunt No.8).

STEPS IN LEARNING

1. You should at least have learned controlled bounces, sit drops, hands-and-knees drops, and front drops before learning this little combination stunt.

2. Do a low backward-leaning sit drop and after you land on your seat, push with the hands and move your upper body forward. As the trampoline lifts you, keep the forward bend at the waist, bend your knees, and reach your hands toward the bed. Drop to a hands-and-knees landing and then rebound to your feet.

3. Go through the same actions as described in Step 2, but instead of coming to your feet after the hands-and-knees landing, bounce up from your hands-and-knees, keeping level as you do so, open out to the front

landing, and from there bounce to a stand.

4. Now, as the final step, simply eliminate the intervening hands-and-knees landing between the sit and the front landings and you have accomplished your objective. Keeping the knees straight all the way will take a little extra practice but will make the stunt look much sharper.

CORRECTION OF ERRORS

A. A failure to rotate far enough forward from your sit position to get a level, flat, front landing is most likely a result of insufficient backward lean on the sit. Other errors which could cause the same result are: (1) not using the arm push coming from the sit position; (2) not swinging the trunk forward strongly enough from the sit; (3) not doubling up or bending enough between the sit and front landings; and (4) not staying bent or doubled up long enough before opening to the front.

a) After the sit landing, forward rotation b) Legs are swinging backward, body c) In position for the front landing. Re-
started.   straightening.   bound from front to feet finishes
                                                                                        stunt.

Fig. 12.   Sit drop to front drop.

B. Inability to come up easily to the feet after the front landing can sometimes be cured by increasing the height, by pushing sooner and harder with the forearms and hands, or by maintaining contact between the hands and the bed for a longer time, sliding the hands backward while pushing them downward against the bed.

Stunt No. 13—FRONT DROP TO SIT DROP

DESCRIPTION OF ACTION. The take-off into this stunt and the first landing are just the same as for the plain front drop (Stunt No.8). When rebounding from the front landing, it is necessary to push with the arms and hands with more force and for a longer time to obtain sufficient backward rotation to swing clear through to a sit drop before bouncing to the feet (Figs. 13a and 13b). The legs should be kept straight and the feet pointed during the entire stunt except that on this front landing, as on most front landings, the knees are bent. The sit should be backward leaning with arms bent in order to be in the best position from which to rebound (Fig. 13c).

STEPS IN LEARNING

1. Before trying this combination you should be able to do well at least the controlled bounces, sit drops, and front drops. Learning each of the twelve preceding stunts in the order listed is, of course, the recommended procedure.

2. In your early attempts you may find it necessary to double up the legs as well as to bend at the waist in order to get enough backward rotation to come from the front landing to the sit. Keep working for the straight leg form.

CORRECTION OF ERRORS. The important defect characteristic of this stunt is the failure to get sufficient backward spin coming from the front to the sit landing. This can be a result of one or all of the following errors.

A. Coming down chest first on the front landing. The knees should land somewhat before the chest if you want to get the maximum backward rotation from this landing.

B. Delaying the downward push. The pressure with your forearms against the bed should begin as soon as they land.

C. Abbreviating the downward push. You should continue the downward pressure, sliding your hands back along the bed as you are leaving the front position, and starting to bend for the sit.

D. Not enough height. It is necessary to do a fairly high bounce before the front drop in order to be able to get the legs through easily, keeping straight knees all the way between the front and

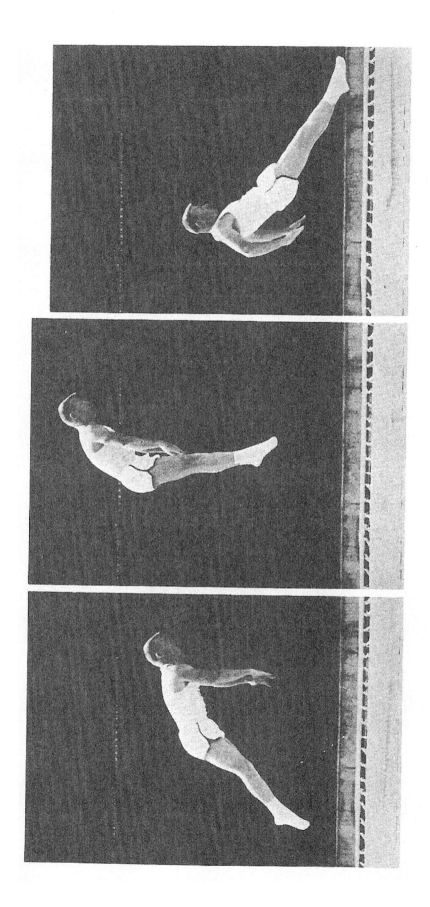

a) After the front landing. The hand b) The legs are swinging forward to- c) Just before the sit landing. Bounce
push has started backward rotation. ward the sit position. to a stand-up will follow.

Fig. 13. Front drop to sit drop.

sit landings.

E. Letting the feet hit. The knees should be allowed to bend as the front-drop contact is made. Bending the knees on the front landing may appear to be a breach of form; but when you keep them straight, the feet make contact with the bed, checking the backward rotation and making it considerably more difficult to complete the stunt. Avoiding this error becomes even more important in later similar stunts.

Stunt No. 14—HALF TWIST TO BACK DROP

DESCRIPTION OF ACTION. Your take-off into this stunt is very much the same as for the front drop (Stunt No.8) with the same slight forward tilt and the same slight forward bend at the waist. During this action your arms assume a wide position, your legs are held straight and together and your feet are pointed. During the lifting portion of the stunt a very little twist is started with the upper body, usually to the left (Fig. 14a). As you reach the peak of the jump you swing one arm (usually the right arm) down and across, past the knees, increasing the shoulder turn in the same direction; i.e., to the left (Fig. 14b). During this turn your body stays nearly straight and your eyes continue to look at the original spot on the bed until your turn is well under way. Finally, to finish the action, you turn the head, bend at the waist and come to a straight-knee back landing (Fig. 14c). You recover to your feet by straightening out at the waist as the trampoline lifts you into the air.

STEPS IN LEARNING

1. As prerequisites to this stunt, you should be able to do the controlled bounces, front drops, and straight-knee back drops. You would do well to have learned also many of the other stunts already described.

2. In order to learn the twisting action at a low height you can learn a knee drop into a front landing and then try the half twist action from the knee drop turning over to a back landing.

3. When you first try this twist from your feet, be sure to keep it low and remember that too little forward rotation is better than too much.

CORRECTION OF ERRORS

A. Overturning the landing, thus landing on the neck instead of the back, can be corrected by tipping forward less at the beginning of the stunt and keeping straight longer during the twist before bending for the landing.

B. Eccentricity in the twist and crookedness on the landing can be eliminated by delaying the head twist and keeping the body nearly straight while twisting.

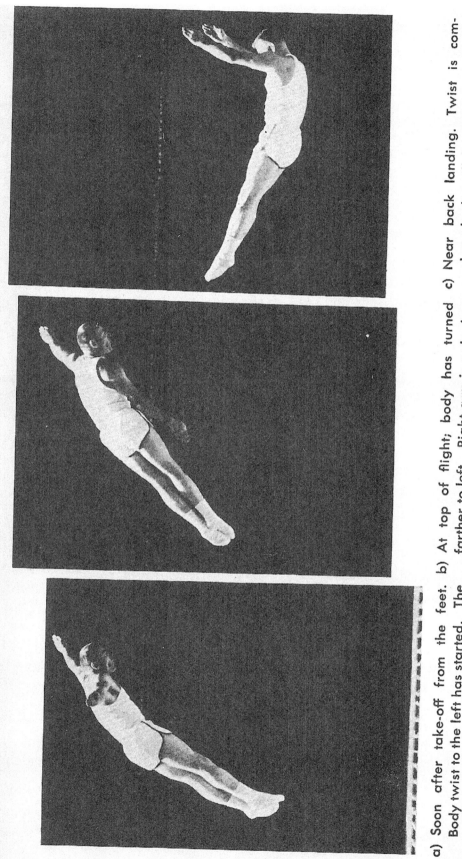

a) Soon after take-off from the feet. b) At top of flight; body has turned c) Near back landing. Twist is com-
Body twist to the left has started. The   farther to left. Right arm is swinging   plete; body will bend more at waist
spread arms and the head have not   past knees across body; head has not   before landing. Return to the feet
started to twist.   yet turned.   will be as in straight knee back drop.

Fig. 14. Half twist to back drop.

C. Twisting right off the mat is another error that spoils the appearance of the stunt. To eliminate this fault go to the other extreme on a few attempts, trying to delay the arm throw and body twist until the latest possible moment.

D. If after executing the twist properly and landing on the back there is difficulty in rebounding to the feet, the cause may be found in an improper relaxing of the knees on the back landing. The knees should be kept straight and the recovery to the feet made as in the straight knee back drop (Stunt No.7). A semi-kick-out style recovery can be substituted by bending the knees before landing on the back and straightening them at the moment of impact.

Stunt No. 15—BACK DROP TO FRONT DROP

DESCRIPTION OF ACTION. Since the kick-out back drop (Stunt No. 9) is recommended for the back drop in this combination, the first actions are those described for that stunt. The kick-out from the back landing however, is made in a more forward and less vertical direction than when the intention is to return to the feet for the second landing (Fig. 15a).

The forward-upward kick-out to a straight-knee and open-at-the-waist position is followed by an immediate bending at the waist into a piked position (Fig. 15b). This position is held as in the sit drop to front drop until your body rotates forward to a position where you can open to a straight and flat front landing (Fig. 15c), from which to rebound to your feet.

STEPS IN LEARNING

1. The prerequisite stunts are controlled bounces, sit drops, hands-and-knees drops, front drops and kick-out back drops. It is recommended that you also be able to do most of the other 14 stunts already described.

2. After reviewing some kick-out back drops, try a few in which you kick at a little lower angle, then double up part way again and land on your hands-and-knees instead of on your feet.

3. When you have Step 2 well in hand, it is a simple matter to maintain your doubled up position (ready for a hands-and-knees landing) until you are nearly ready to land, then open out to land on the front instead.

4. With a little more preliminary height and a little more force, you can get enough clearance to get through to your front landing with your knees kept perfectly straight and your feet pointed during the time between the end of the kick-out and the slightly bent-knee front landing.

CORRECTION OF ERRORS

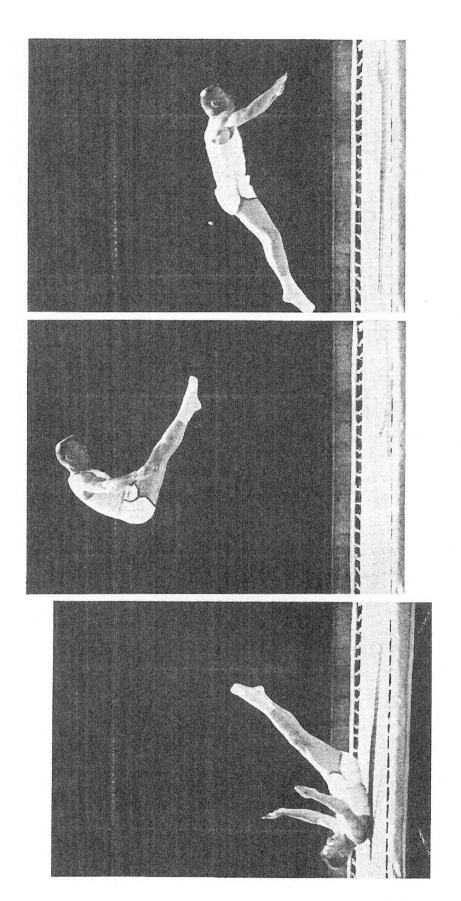

a) Leaving the bed after dropping in a tucked position and kicking out, as in Figs. 9a, 9b, and 9c.

b) Turning forward by bending forward at the waist, following the stretch out begun in Fig. 15a.

c) Opening from the bent body turning position to the straight front landing position. Rebound to the feet will follow.

Fig. 15.   Back drop to front drop.

A. Underturning so that you are not getting quite over to your flat front landing or so that you are finding it necessary to bend your knees in order to get far enough over may be a result of kicking too vertically on the kick-out or more likely of a poorly timed or incomplete kick-out from the back landing. A review of the technique which you learned for the kick-out back drop (Stunt No.9) and some practice on that stunt would be appropriate. Now, when you try again to do the back drop to front drop be sure that you use the same timing, kick at a somewhat lower angle, and do not start bending forward to speed up the forward rotation until the kick-out has been completed.

B. Overturning the front landing may be caused by kicking at too low an angle. Try a more nearly vertical kick.

C. The amount of time you hold your bent position before opening to the front landing is an important element of control. Hold the bend longer to correct an underturn, hold it more briefly to correct an overturn.

Stunt No. 16—FRONT DROP TO BACK DROP

DESCRIPTION OF ACTION. The first action of this stunt is identical to that described for the front drop (Stunt No.8) and it continues much like the action described for the front drop to sit drop (Stunt No. 12). On the rebound from the front the push with the hands is strong and extensive (Fig. 16a), the knees are brought up to the chest into a tucked position (without grasping shins), and the chin is dropped to the chest (Fig. 16b). This tucked position is held until the back makes contact with the bed (Fig. 16c), then the legs and body are extended in time to help push the bed deeper and thereby increase the lift given the body to enable it to regain the standing position. This last part is the kick-out back drop action, described for Stunt NO.9.

STEPS IN LEARNING

1. As with all the stunts in this book, the order in which they are presented is a good order in which to learn them. It is all right, however, to learn the stunts out of order if you prefer, but be sure that you have the minimum prerequisites before you proceed. In this case, the stunts required to be learned before this front drop to back drop would be the controlled bounce, the front drop, the front drop to sit drop, and the kick-out back drop.

2. After reviewing the prerequisite stunts, you can proceed directly to an attempt at the whole stunt without any other preliminaries. At first you may prefer not to attempt to use the kick-out from the back landing, but instead be content with getting to the back in the right position. After a few of these, you should be able to add the kick-out and thereby recover to a standing finish.

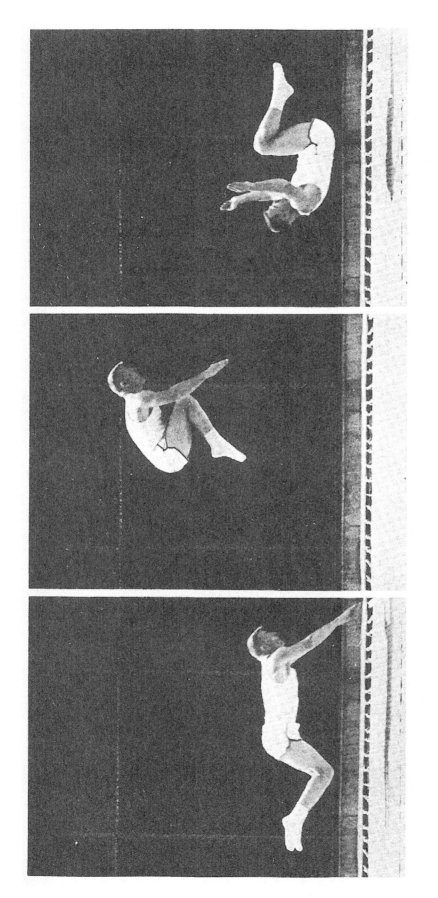

a) After the front landing. Hands have pushed down. Body and knees starting to bend. Backward rotation started.

b) The doubled-up position has been quickly assumed to speed up backward turning.

c) Near the back landing. Tuck position continues. Kick-out will follow the back landing and bring trampolinist back to standing position.

Fig. 16. Front drop to back drop.

CORRECTION OF ERRORS

A. Inability to get through far enough after the front landing to hit correctly on the back is the most common difficulty. Increasing the height of the preliminary bounces and the drop to the front may help. Also you will find it helps to land a little bit knees-before-chest instead of chest-before-knees to get the maximum backward rotation from the front landing. Additionally, having the arms in the correct position on the front landing, starting their push early, making it forceful, and continuing it as long as possible will help. Forcefully bringing the knees to the chest with legs bent, and dropping the chin to the chest can add to the backward rotation.

B. Overturning on the back drop and landing on the neck instead of the back is not nearly as common an error as underturning but one that should be quickly corrected when it does occur. A little less bouncing height into the front drop or less arm-and-hand push from the front landing will prevent the overturn, as would a less tightly tucked turning position.

Stunt No. 17—HALF TWIST TO FRONT DROP

DESCRIPTION OF ACTING. The initial lift for this stunt is much like that described for the sit drop (Stunt No.4), in that your body is tipped backward by thrusting your hips forward and pulling your shoulders backward. In this stunt, however, your hip thrust and shoulder pull are considerably stronger and therefore your backward rotation is greater. In addition, there is also a twisting action of your hips as they are thrust forward. Your head remains facing the original direction until the height of the lift is reached and your hips have been twisted part way around (Fig. 17a). At the peak and during the downward flight your head and shoulders follow the twisting action started with your hips, twisting around, until you are facing the bed (Fig. 17b). Your body which has been kept straight during the twist may be flexed at the waist a little bit to prepare for the front landing (Fig. 17c). The front landing and the rebound to the feet are the same as you have previously learned for the front drop (Stunt No.8).

STEPS IN LEARNING

1. The necessary prerequisite stunts include the controlled bounces, the sit drop, and the front drop. Especially recommended for additional background are the back drop and the twisting stunts (Stunts Nos. 11 and 14).

2. In order to get the feel of this particular style of twist, you can try it most easily as part of a feet-to-feet bounce. Without doing any tipping backward, you can twist your lower body as you take off from the bed on one of your bounces. When you are about half way through the bounce, turn your head and shoulders to follow the twist you started with your hips. This should

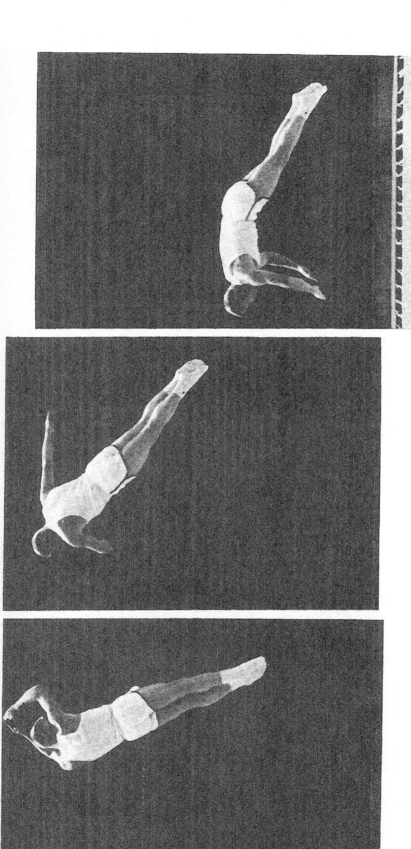

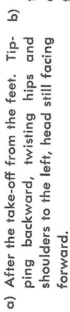

a) After the take-off from the feet. Tipping backward, twisting hips and shoulders to the left, head still facing forward.

b) Body continues left twist. Head has turned to follow the twist. Arms dropping down closer to body to aid twist.

c) Twist completed; body bent slightly to level off. Front landing will follow and lead to rebound to the feet.

Fig. 17. Half twist to front drop.

result in landing on your feet facing somewhere near the direction opposite from your starting position.

3. When Step 2 has been fairly well learned, your next problem is to get the right amount of backward tip in the stunt to come to a horizontal plane while accomplishing the twist. In going through the trial-and-error stage in regard to the amount of backward rotation, it would be best for you to substitute the hands-and-knees landing for the front landing because you can absorb errors this way more comfortably.

4. Practice until you consistently are able to get the forward-thrust hips to lead the twist, the head and shoulders to follow later, and to hold this open position until you are turned around face down and then make a quick change to a level hands-and-knees landing. Now you are ready to do the entire stunt by eliminating the hands-and-knees position going into the front landing instead.

CORRECTION OF ERRORS

A. Turning your head and shoulders immediately into the twist will lead to an inferior kind of twist and a less good-looking position. If you seem to be making this error, you should review the hips-first twist motion standing on the floor and also on the bounce as in Step 2 above.

B. A failure to get enough backward tip is caused by an insufficiently vigorous forward thrust of your hips during the take-off and results in a landing that is "short" of horizontal or results in having to use an extreme bend in the latter part of the stunt to prevent the landing.

C. Being short of twist will result in a landing partly on your side instead of clear over onto the front. If this is happening, you probably are restraining your hip twist by doing it too late or too gently, or possibly you are being too strict about not letting your shoulders follow the twist soon enough.

Stunt No. 18—HALF TWIST FROM BACK DROP

DESCRIPTION OF 'ACTION. This stunt is an ordinary back drop with a half twist executed after the back landing before returning to your feet. The kick-out back drop is more effective than the straight-knee style for this purpose. The drop part of this twisting stunt, then, is the same as described for Stunt No.9, and the timing and direction of kick-out are also as described there. Your twist, however, must be started at the same time that the kick-out starts. The lower part of your body, below the shoulders starts the twist (Fig. 18a). This is a kind of corkscrew action with the legs and then the hips turning over as the legs are extended and the body opened out (Fig. 18b). When the lift of the bed, amplified by the well-timed twisting kick-out, has gotten you into the air and you are approaching the

a) This hip-twisting kick-out from the back landing follows the tucked drop to the back (shown in Figs. 9a and 9b).

b) The horizontally stretched body has completed half of its twist. The head has not yet been turned.

c) The turn of the head and drop of the arms has nearly completed the twist. The body and knees bend to help attain the stand-up finish.

Fig. 18.   Half twist from back drop.

highest point of your flight, turn your head and shoulders in the same direction as the hips have already turned, completing the half twist (Fig. 18c). At approximately this same time, it will be necessary (if you have aimed your kick at a high enough angle) to bend somewhat at the waist, and possibly a little at the knees, in order to bring your feet down toward the bed and put you in a stand-up position for landing.

STEPS IN LEARNING

1. The learning of this stunt must be preceded by the learning of the kick-out back drop, which in turn follows upon the straight-knee back drop, sit drop and the controlled bounces.

2. A review of the kick-out back drop, making sure of the timing of the kick and the high direction of the kick, just before trying this twisting variation will be helpful.

3. To get the feel of the corkscrew-type hip twist, lie on your back in the correct tucked position and have a helper stand over you, take hold of your legs and lift and twist as you slowly extend, as in the kick-out action. You can do a similar practice exercise without an assistant by mildly bouncing up and down on the trampoline in the tucked kicked-out back drop position; then on one of the lifts, kick all the way out with the hip twist and try to land fully extended on the back and side.

4. Now, with the idea of the twist learned, reread the instructions for the completed stunt and give it a full-fledged try. It might be well to have someone at the side of the trampoline in case you go crooked on your first attempts.

CORRECTION OF ERRORS

A. Unless you have the kick-out back drop skills and timing well established as habits, the attempt to add the twist may cause you to make one or more of the errors described for that stunt. Check back through the instructions for the kick-out back drop to correct these errors.

B. Going crooked and landing off center or even off the bed is not an uncommon error. This results from a too early rolling so that when you land on your back or at least before you leave that position you have rolled somewhat toward the direction of your twist and consequently the actual direction of your kick-out is not straight-up-the-middle, as it should be. To correct, be sure you have picked a target spot straight forward-upward and continue to aim at that spot with your kick-out and with your sight until you are stretched out above the trampoline bed.

C. An incomplete stretch-out, keeping some bend at the waist or at the knees, can also result in crookedness or an incomplete twist or both. Extend as if trying to touch the ceiling or the moon with your toes before turning the head and bending for the downward flight.

OTHER ELEMENTARY TWISTS AND COMBINATIONS TO TRY:

1. Knee drop to sit drop to feet

2. Front drop, half twist to back drop, to feet (shoulders lead twist, head delays)

3. Half twist from straight-knee back drop to feet (hips lead, head and

shoulders delay)

4. Half twist to back drop, half twist to feet

5. Half twist from front drop to feet (turn head and shoulders early)

6. Half twist to front drop, half twist to feet

7. Sit drop, half twist to front drop (hips lead twist, head and shoulders delay)

8. Back drop, half twist to front drop (hips lead twist)

9. Sit drop, to back drop, to feet

10. Half twist from sit drop to feet (shoulders lead twist, head delays,

arms reach overhead)

11. Back pullover to sit drop

12. Back pullover to back pullover

13. Back pullover to front drop

14. Front drop to back pullover

4

Common Knick-Knacks

If you have learned to perform a good portion of the stunts already described and possibly tried a few of the extra ones listed at the end of Chapter 3, you are ready to go on to these next five, commonly done, stunts which we call knick-knacks. They are a little more difficult than the preceding stunts and need to be learned with careful progression if they are going to be done correctly.

Stunt No. 19—SWIVEL HIPS (Sit Drop, Half Twist, Sit Drop)

DESCRIPTION OF ACTION. The first part of this stunt is a drop to a sit landing, as shown and described under Stunt No. 4. From your backward- leaning sit landing, a strong push with your arms and the forward swing of your trunk assist the trampoline to lift you upward with a forward rotation (Fig. 19a). As you are being lifted, you must swing your arms overhead, turning your shoulders and trunk about a quarter-turn to the left or right and straightening out at your waist to a fully stretched position at the peak of your lift (Fig. 19b). Your head does not turn during this first part of the body turn but continues to look in the same direction as at the beginning until after the peak of the stunt. On the way down you continue to turn, drop your arms, bring your head around a half-turn, bend at the waist and prepare to land in a sit drop position facing opposite to your original direction (Fig. 19c). From the sit drop, a rebound to the feet landing completes your stunt. The knees remain straight through the entire action.

STEPS IN LEARNING

1. You should first of all be able to bounce in good form, balance, and control (Stunt No. 1). You need to be adept at doing good, high, backward-leaning sit drops with proper landing and rebound (Stunt No. 4). You need also to be able to do the half twist to sit drop (Stunt No. 10). All the other previous eighteen

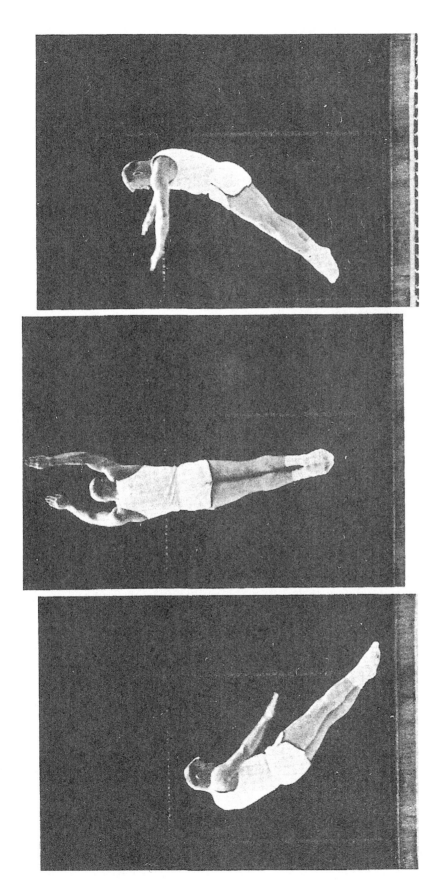

a) After the sit landing on the way up b) Mid-way in the stunt with 90 degrees c) With the twist completed. Preparing into the twist. of twist accomplished. for the second sit landing.

Fig. 19. Swivel hips.

stunts would also be helpful background.

2. Do several sit drops in which you swing your arms vigorously overhead and straighten the body forcefully as you leave the sitting position, and land in a hands-overhead, arched-body stand.

3. Next try a sit drop coming up to a quarter-turned, straight-body stand with hands high overhead and with the head still facing the same direction as it started. Practice this until you can do it well.

4. Now, starting from the position in which you finished (body facing sideward, arms over head, head still forward), jump into the air, tipping toward the direction in which you are looking, turning the shoulders another quarter turn in a continuing direction; then, bending at the waist and turning the head and dropping the hands, make a sit drop landing, rebounding to a stand. Repeat this until it feels smooth and easy. Except that you start with the quarter-turn already accomplished, this step is done just like Stunt No. 10, the half twist to sit drop.

5. You are ready now to try doing Step 3 and then, as you land on your feet, bounce immediately into Step 4. Do this combination several times.

6. With a little more height before the first sit landing and a little more forward rotation from it, you will be able to do Step 5 without touching the bed with your feet between the quarter twisting lift and the quarter twist to sit. This, then, is the completed swivel hips.

CORRECTION OF ERRORS

A. If you find yourself turning around in a bent-at-the-waist (sort of sitting) position, practice Step 2 again to re-emphasize the immediate straightening, stretching, arching action after the sit drop.

B. If you have trouble getting your legs through straight and getting a flat sit landing on your second sit, your trouble may be not enough backward lean before the first sit or not enough forward lunge after the sit. Practice Step 2, emphasizing the backward-leaning sit and trying to get a forward-leaning stretch-stand finish.

C. Increased height, holding the stretch as long as possible, and delaying the head turn will help make this a smooth, even turn rather than a snappy or jerky movement.

Stunt No. 20—Half Turntable (Front Drop, Half Turn, Front Drop)

DESCRIPTION OF ACTION. The first portion of a half turntable is simply a forward-tipping, semi-jackknife drop to a front landing as described for the front drop (Stunt No. 7). During the uplift of the trampoline bed immediately after the lowest point of the bed's depression, you must start the downward and sideward pressure of the forearms and hands and the sideward turn of the head, looking around over your shoulder (Fig. 20a). As your body begins to leave the bed, the strong head turn is accompanied by a turn of the shoulders by bending sideways at the waist and along the trunk. At about the same time, your body bends sharply forward at the waist into a jackknife position with the hands passing close to the feet (Fig. 20b). This compact position is held until you get turned around so that you are facing the other end of the trampoline You open the jackknife, dropping to the front landing (Fig. 20c), and rebound to a standing position as in the recovery from an ordinary front drop. This turn from one front drop to another is not a twist around the long axis of the body, but instead is a turning around as if on a turntable keeping the front side toward the trampoline at all times.

STEPS IN LEARNING

1. Although all of the preceding stunts can very well come before this one in your learning progression, there are a few of them that most certainly must. Controlled bounces, hands-and-knees drops, and front drops are definite prerequisites.

2. To learn the jackknife position for turning, it is well to try dropping to your front landing and from it going immediately into a jackknife position without turning or standing up. The second landing then is in a "pyramid" position, facing the same way as the front landing. The pyramid position is with hands and feet landing on the bed at the same time and with the body bent and legs straight so that the hands are fairly close to the feet and the hips are high in the air.

3. To learn the turning action you do the same kind of drop to the front landing, then as you are being lifted you turn your head, push away with the hands and bend at the waist to land in the pyramid landing facing the side of the trampoline. Thus you will have done a 90-degree turn which is just half of your eventual goal.

4. You can now work this turn around on successive tries until you can land in the pyramid position facing opposite to your starting direction.
That will be the half-turn (180 degrees).

5. After you are able repeatedly to complete the half-turn as in Step 4 and land on hands and feet, the next step is to change at the last moment from the jackknife position to the open position and land in the front landing position instead of the pyramid position. Complete the stunt by bouncing up to a stand.

a) Just after the front landing. Starting lateral turn and body bend.

b) With half of the turn finished, the jack-knife position is complete.

c) Opening to the second front landing as the turn is completed.

Fig. 20. Half turntable.

CORRECTION OF ERRORS

A. There is a tendency when learning the half turntable to push down too hard with the arms and hands when leaving the front landing, and to rotate backward as if going to a back drop but at the same time turn over laterally to land on the front again. This may get you to the same place, but is not a turntable motion. Instead, you must push only a little downward and a lot sideward, your head must swing out and toward the edge of the bed and thence around to the rear. The head must stay low, relatively near the bed, during the turn.

B. Bending the knees, going into a semi-tuck position during the turn is not so much an error as an alternate form for the half turntable. It is probably less good-looking, but equally as effective. The learning procedure for this type would involve substituting hands-and-knees landings in place of the pyramid landings in the preparatory phases.

C. Failure to get enough turn to land squarely 180 degrees around from the start is usually due to not emphasizing the looking around (leading with the head) or to not turning it at the right time. Other possible
causes are insufficient sideward push with arms and hands when leaving the front landing and incomplete bending or jackknifing in the turn.

Stunt No. 21—BARREL ROLL (Sit Drop, Full Twist, Sit Drop)

DESCRIPTION OF ACTION. To do a barrel roll, you start out with a good layout drop to a sit landing, making particularly sure that your landing is backward leaning with your arms bent. As the bed starts its upward lift, you do not lunge forward with the trunk as in your previously learned sit drop stunts, but instead you keep the backward lean and push hard with both arms. As you are leaving the bed, you lift your midsection and hips forward and twist them strongly to right or left. This early and strong twist of your hips in the layout position is not accompanied immediately by a shoulder and head twist (Fig. 21a). They remain briefly in the forward direction. When approaching the highest point of this lift , the shoulders and head are forcefully turned to catch up with the hips and then lead the rest of the full twist (Fig. 21b). The arms, after their strong push, may be either held down at the sides during the twist, doubled in tight across the chest, lifted to an overhead reach, or the leading arm may go straight overhead while the other wraps across the body. In any case, the arms must be kept in close to the axis of the twist and the body must be kept straight in order to twist most efficiently. After the twist is complete, you come to a second sit landing which is in the same direction and the same position as the first (Fig. 21c). A little forward lunge and hand push after this second sit will serve to bring you to a stand on the rebound.

a) Following the first sit landing. The b) At the high point. Straight body roll c) Approaching the second sit landing.
hip twist and body roll are well   half-finished.   Body roll nearly complete.
started.

Fig. 21. Barrel roll.

STEPS IN LEARNING

1. The chances of learning the barrel roll easily and correctly are probably best if you have already learned the preceding 20 stunts. However, the only stunts that you should consider as necessary prerequisites are controlled bounces and sit drops. The front drop and especially the half twist to front drop (Stunt No. 17) are highly recommended for background.

2. From a sitting position on the trampoline bed, rise to a one-arm leaning support. In this position, the body is straight with the hips twisted on past the rest of the body. The feet are on the bed and also the hand of the supporting arm (left, if twist is to the left). The supporting arm is straight and the other arm is extended toward the ceiling. Keep your head in the forward-looking position, as in the original sit position. Don't try to stay in this position long for it is a difficult balance. To get the roll, you throw the arm across the body as you release the support of the arm. You keep your body straight and spin around to a flat-back landing. The rise from the sit and the spin to the back can be done in immediate succession after a little practice.

3. Starting from a bouncing sit position and otherwise doing Step 2 with a minimum of time between its two parts will give you the feel of the principle motion of the barrel roll. Substitute a low sit drop for the bouncing sits and you have the barrel roll practically made.

4. A somewhat different progression in learning the barrel roll involves using the drop-to-a-sit landing right from the beginning. The first step is to learn to do a drop to the sit, then lift, leaning backward and straightening out at the waist, then bend again to the second backward leaning sit landing and bounce to a stand. This is in effect a barrel roll without the roll.

5. The second step in this alternate progression is to put a hip twist into the lift from the sit, but not follow with the head and shoulders. The hips can be more or less twisted back again for the second sit landing.

6. Now finally you can put, in a stronger hip twist and then follow with the head and shoulders and arm action until you can get enough twist to do the entire stunt.

CORRECTION OF ERRORS

A. The most common error is not staying back when leaving the first sit landing with the result that the second sit landing is done leaning forward or even with feet hitting first. The exercise in Step 4, above, should be practiced more.

B. A second common error is leading the twist with an early head-and-shoulders twist instead of an early hip-twist and a delayed head-and-shoulder twist. This results in a different and, in my opinion, an inferior type of twist.

C. When your twist is too weak, you either fail to get around far enough to sit or you are forced to bend into your sit before you have completed the twist and will therefore be sitting crooked on the bed with the feet pointed off at an angle instead of straight down the middle. To amplify twist, emphasize the strong push of both hands accompanied by an immediate and forceful hip twist, and be straight while twisting.

Stunt No. 22—EARLY TWISTING CRADLE
(Back Drop, Half Twist, Back Drop)

DESCRIPTION OF ACTION. Using the same technique you learned for a kick-out back drop (Stunt No. 9), drop to your back and as you are landing start your kick-out action to give you a forceful rebound. This opening action is different from that used in the ordinary kick-out back drop in two ways. For one thing, you should kick at a lower angle to give more forward rotation. Far another, you are to twist your legs and hips in a corkscrew action as you kick (Fig. 22a). This corkscrew kick is the same as learned for the half twist from back drop (Stunt No. 18). As in that stunt, you delay the head turn, letting the twist extend to the shoulder area as the body is stretched out more or less horizontally above the bed. After your greatest height has been reached and you are starting down again, turn the head quickly and tuck up, bending both at the knees and at the waist (Fig. 22b). You now drop to a second kick-out back drop-this time facing the opposite direction (Fig. 22c). A well-timed kick-out will give you a good lift to enable you to come to your feet for the final landing.

STEPS IN LEARNING

1. The cradle is the most difficult stunt we have considered up to now.
Having learned a considerable number of the previously listed stunts therefore will make it more likely that you can get this one without undue frustration. The list of stunts which you definitely must have learned includes the controlled bounce, the kick-out back drop, and the half twist from back drop.

2. After reviewing your kick-out back drop and the half twist from back drop, learn to do a quarter-twist from the back landing, finishing on your feet with your body facing the side of the trampoline and your head facing the same direction as at the start of the drop.

3. As another preliminary stunt, begin from the standing position in which you finished Step 2, above, jump into the air tipping toward the direction you are looking (towards your right shoulder if you are twisting to the left), continuing the twist in the same direction as you started. After you are in the air, turn

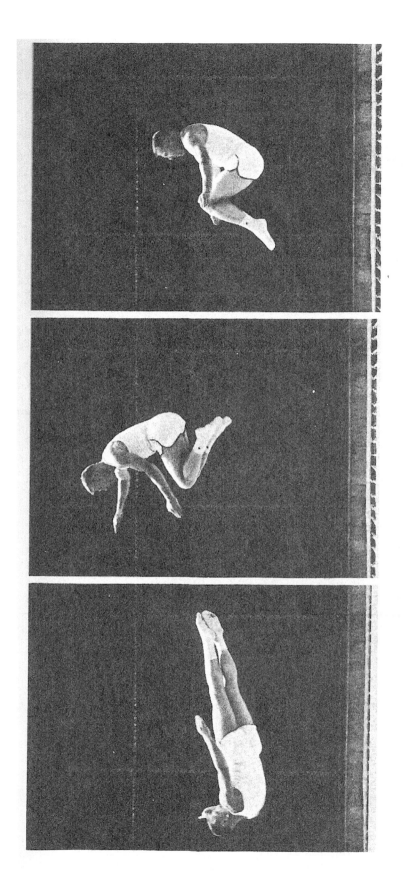

a) The hip-twisting kick-out, following the first back landing. The drop to the back was in a doubled-up position.

b) Following the twisting stretch, the head turns and the body and knees bend.

c) Approaching the second back landing. Another kick-out will bring about recovery to the feet.

Fig. 22. Early twisting cradle.

your head around toward the other end of the trampoline, double up into the kick-out position, and drop into what corresponds to your second kick-out back drop action which brings you to a stand-up finish.

4. Practice these two halves of the stunt separately (Steps 2 and 3), and then start working on combining them into two consecutive moves with the landing on the feet after the first (Step 2) just long enough to take an immediate rebound lift into the second half (Step 3).

5. Now to eliminate the feet-landing between the two halves of the stunt, the direction of the original kick-out must be at a little lower angle to provide a little more forward rotation. A little more height preceding the first drop may also be helpful. At any rate, you need to develop the skill of going through Step 2 right up to the point of landing, then quickly changing into the head-turned, body-tucked position for the second back drop without ever letting the feet touch the bed. When you can do this, you have it made.

CORRECTION OF ERRORS

A. Errors in the landing positions for the first back drop and in the timing of the kick-out action will not occur if the back drop itself has been sufficiently well learned (see Stunt No. 9).

B. Failure to fully extend the body on the first twisting kick-out and failure to ride that extension as long as possible results in an inferior cradle and oftentimes in an inability to get enough twist to land squarely on the back after the twist.

C. Turning the head around at about the same time as you are doing the
first kick-out is a serious error that results in a poorer style and often in either a crookedness or weakness of the kick-out.

D. Kicking off sideways is a result of anticipating the twist by rolling the body on the first back landing so that even when you kick straight ahead in relation to your body, it is off to the side in relation to the trampoline. Stay squarely on your back, keep looking forward, and kick out at a target which is down the middle.

Stunt No. 23—LATE TWISTING CRADLE

DESCRIPTION OF ACTION. This stunt like the early twisting cradle (No. 22) is a back drop, half twist, back drop. The principle difference is in the manner in which the twist is accomplished. The twist in the early twisting cradle is started by the hips as we have seen. The twist in the late twisting cradle is started with the arms, head, and shoulders; and, of course, as the name implies, the twist comes later in the stunt. The drop-to-the-back landing is the same as you use in Stunts Nos. 9 and 15. The kick-out is forward and upward without any twisting action. The direction of the kick is fairly low as though the objective were to rotate forward with almost straight body to a front landing. As the kick-out carries the body into a fairly straight-body position rotating forward, the arms should be swung wide laterally (Fig. 23a). As you are passing the midway point where you are more or less standing up straight on thin air a little way above the bed, you begin the twist action. In order to twist, you swing one arm (your right if you are going to twist to the left) vigorously down past your knee and across your body, thereby starting your shoulder turn (Fig. 23b). Your head comes around now also, just after the arm throw. This puts you into a position to land on your back (Fig. 23c). If you are simply going to bounce to your feet after the second back drop, the straight-knee back drop form is best. If you are going to attempt a second consecutive cradle immediately from this back-chop ending of the first, the kick-out style of landing and rebound is better. To be in a position to go into the tuck position before landing on the back in order to use the kick-out, you want to be a little less far over on your rotation; therefore you must use a little higher angle in your original kick-out.

STEPS IN LEARNING

1. The necessary preliminary stunts for this late twisting cradle are the controlled bounces, the straight-knee back drop, the kick-out back drop, the half twist to back drop (Stunt No. 14), and the back drop to front drop (Stunt No. 15). Considerable experience with most of the other 22 stunts that precede this one is also recommended as a preparation.

2. From a low bounce, go into a kick-out back drop, aiming the kick at a lowish angle, straightening out immediately and come to a stand-up landing with the arms spread. Immediately rebound, tipping forward toward a front drop. Throw the arm across, turning the shoulders and then the head, going through the motions you use for the half twist to back drop (Stunt No. 14). From the straight-knee back landing, open at the waist to recover to a stand.

3. By taking a little more height before the original drop and possibly a little more force on the kick-out, you will be able to eliminate the landing on the feet but will pass through a position in the air in which you are standing a little above the bed and going over toward a front landing with the arms out sideward. Throwing the arms across, turning the shoulders, then the head, and bending at the waist (as you did in Step 2 after the midway landing) will put you into your straight-knee back drop landing and rebound to feet.

4. In order to learn to do the alternative style, using the kick-out back drop landing after the twist, go back to Step 2 and try it with this difference. As you are rebounding from the midpoint stand-up landing, you must tip forward less so that, after you do

a) After the back landing, a kick-out and sit-up have started forward rotation.

b) Body straightening and cross-body arm throw begins the shoulder and body twist.

c) With the twist nearly complete. Preparing for the second back landing. To be followed by rebound to a stand.

Fig. 23. Late twisting cradle.

the twist, you will need to tuck up in order to get far enough over to do the back drop. This puts you in the right position for the kick-out recovery from the back drop. This same result can be accomplished in Step 3 by making your original kick at a higher angle in order to limit the forward rotation and make it necessary to double up after you twist in order to get to the back landing.

CORRECTION OF ERRORS

A. If you are twisting at the time indicated and are using plenty of arm throw but are still not getting around easily on your half-twist, it is permissible to edge into your twist a little. This means that as you are getting your kick-out, and you are riding over with the arms out, you can already be twisting a little bit. The twist becomes obvious when the arm throw and then the head turn speed it up.

B. To correct yourself on either of the most common errors of twisting too soon or of not straightening out before twisting, you would do well to practice Step 2 in the learning procedure, emphasizing the correction of your error.

C. This is an easy stunt on which to get sloppy habits of form. Attention to pointed feet will enhance the appearance and attention to straight, closed legs and stretched body will not only improve the looks of this stunt, but give you a nice start on the corkscrew (Stunt No.3 36).

The five stunts described in detail in this chapter are representative of a group of stunts that are easy to try, but tricky to accomplish and difficult to do really well. Chapter 6 describes another group of similar stunts that are on a somewhat higher level of difficulty and which are both more difficult and more treacherous to try. Before you start working on them, you will probably want to make some real progress with some of the forward somersault work in Chapter 5. If, however, before or during your somersault learning, you want some more stunts like the preceding five, it would be perfectly all right to proceed cautiously with the stunts in Chapter 6. I suggest first of all, however, that you might try using these five stunts from Chapter 4 in multiples of two or three or more, swinging right from one into another of the same stunt. Also you will enjoy mixing them up, swinging both into and out of the stunts you have already learned, from and into other different stunts from your repertoire. In addition, may I encourage you to make up new stunts and combinations of landings, similar to the ones described.

Some examples of stunts which we have not described in detail and which will not be covered in later chapters are listed below. Most of them contain elements identical to one or more of the stunts described in detail in this and other chapters of this book. With a little ingenuity and page flipping it should not be too difficult to find or figure out a good way to learn them. Usually it helps to review the stunt most like the new one or on which the new one is based. Then try to learn to do an incomplete version of the new stunt which is between the basic stunt and the one you are trying to learn. You can thus acquire the skill to complete the stunt through a gradual process of increasing the spin, the twist, or the rotation on successive attempts. After you have succeeded in acquiring the ability to do some of the new stunts easily and with good form, you can start combining two or more of them of the same or different varieties into interesting swing time sequences.

MORE EASY KNICK-KNACKS LISTED:

1. Front drop, full twist to front drop, bounce to feet (push down with hand and foot on one side, throw other arm across body and wrap up tightly)

2. Flat back, half turntable, to flat back, bounce to feet (use hand push, then tuck for turn)

3. Partial back pullover with kick-out half twist to back drop, bounce to feet (kick-out nearly straight up with hip-twisting, body-straightening kick)

4. Full twist from feet to sit drop, bounce to feet (body tip is backward, head and shoulders lead the twist, body straight while twisting)

5. Full twist from sit drop to feet (strong push with hands, head and shoulders lead the twist)

6. Full twist to front drop, bounce to feet (forward body tip with arms wide, body straight, late cross-body arm throw and head turn into twist)

7. Back drop, inverted swan, back drop, bounce to feet (almost vertical kick-out, head back during swan)

8. Full twist to back drop, bounce to feet (backward tip, early head and shoulder twist, body straight)

9. Full twist from back drop to feet (from wide-armed back landing throw arm across and turn head)

10. Swivel hips with added half twist to front drop bounce to feet (get extra forward rotation from sit landing)

11. Barrel roll with added half twist to front drop, bounce to feet (more backward lean than for barrel roll)

12. Full twist to sit drop, full twist to feet (combination of NO.4 and NO.5 from this list)

13. Full twist to back drop, full twist to feet (combination of NO.8 and No. 9 from this list)

5

The Forward Somersault Group

Generally speaking, the forward somersault is a stunt in which you spring from your feet, turn completely over forward, and land on your feet again. More specifically, the forward somersault can be done in either a tuck, pike, or layout position and there are various fractions, multiples, and variations of forward turnovers which fall in the forward somersault category and are dealt with in this chapter.

I have postponed the treatment of them until this late in your learning process because I have a healthy respect for the dangers involved in trying to learn them too soon and a conviction that considerable trampoline experience is most helpful as a basis for learning somersaults correctly. If you have looked ahead to this chapter without having taken the time to learn a great many of the stunts described in Chapters 2, 3, and 4, I strongly recommend that, after you have satisfied your curiosity and whetted your appetite by reading about somersaults, you take a few weeks or months to learn to do well a large share of the preceding twenty-three stunts before you start on the forward somersault group.

The first five stunts described in this group are really primarily preparatory stunts leading to the complete forward somersault (Stunt No. 29). They are at the same time good stunts in and of themselves and worthy of separate explanations and separate learning. The last four stunts in this chapter are a few variations of the forward turnover which are most important and not substantially more difficult than the basic tucked forward somersault. At the end of the chapter is a list of additional forward turnover stunts of comparable difficulty which you can work out for yourself if you have mastered all of the nine which have been more completely described.

Stunt No. 24—HANDS-AND-KNEES TURNPIKE
(Hands-and-Knees Drop, Forward Turnover Piked, to Sit Drop)

DESCRIPTION OF ACTION. You go into the air with a little forward tip, bending forward at the waist and bending to a right angle at the knees into a hands-and-knees landing position. The drop is made to the hands-and-knees landing on the bed and as the following upsurge of the bed lifts you up, you continue to support with your straight arms while you straighten your knees, pressing down on the bed with your toes as you do so (Fig. 24a). You also, at the same time, try to increase the bend at the waist and duck your head down forcefully. These actions combine to take you into the air in a forward-traveling, forward-rotating, pike position with the knees straight and feet pointed. As your hands leave the bed, the arms spread out laterally for the open-pike turnover phase of the stunt (Fig. 24b). When you are about three-fourths of the way through the stunt, you open out some at the waist, increasing the angle that the trunk makes with the legs, loosening the pike. At the same time, your arms drop and you reach behind your hips ready for the landing (Fig. 24c). The landing should be in the backward-leaning sit drop position and should result in an easy rebound to a stand.

STEPS IN LEARNING

1. As previously stated, a lot of trampoline experience is a basic requirement for starting this stunt. Some tumbling experience would also be helpful. Specifically, the controlled bounces, the hands-and-knees drop, and the sit drop are necessary prerequisites to the hands-and-knees turnpike.

2. To get the feel of turning over forward, staying straight in line while turning, maintaining the piked position, and coming to a sit finish, do a few repetitions of the following exercise. Stand on the trampoline with the legs spread wide, bend over with knees straight placing the hands on the bed as close in to the line the feet are on as possible. Bend your arms but not your legs, duck your head and roll straight forward onto your back and up to a straight-knee sit position. This should be repeated until there is no tendency to go crooked on the roll.

3. From a stationary hands-and-knees position on the trampoline, straighten the knees forcefully, supporting with the arms, sending the bent hips high up behind. The pointed toes maintain contact as long as they can and as they leave the bed they continue to point at the spot on the bed where they were in contact. When you have reached, and held momentarily, a sort of extremely-piked handstand, you return to the hands-and-knees position. Repeat this exercise a number of times.

4. Starting again from the stationary hands-and-knees position, use the same motion as in Step 3 but instead of continuing to

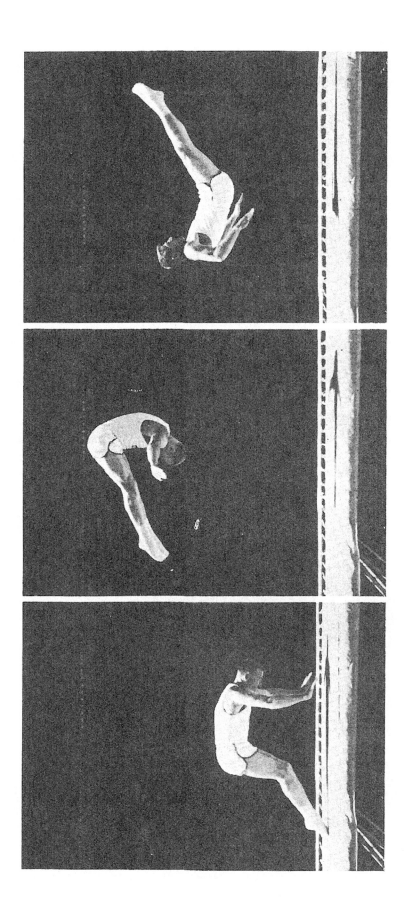

a) Starting into the forward turnover after a hands-and-knees landing. Notice toe-press.

b) Turning over forward in the open-pike position.

c) Opening from the tight pike to sit landing. Bounce to feet will follow.

Fig. 24. Hands-and-knees turnpike.

support with the arms, you give a supporting push as the hips start up, then take the hands off the bed and reach them out toward the sides of the trampoline (open-pike position). At the same time, you duck your head and continue to push against the bed with the pointed feet by continuing to straighten your knees. You land on your back, keeping your knees straight so that they cannot by accident come down and hit you in the face.

5. Now if you will precede the same action used in Step 4 with several hands-and-knees bounces (bouncing up off the bed and down again in the
hands-and-knees position), you will have enough added height to make it around almost to the sitting position.

6. Substitute the hands-and-knees drop for the hands-and-knees bounces and you will have sufficient additional height to turn over easily to the sit landing. This, then, is the completed stunt.

CORRECTION OF ERRORS

A. Bumping your head on the bed after landing on the hands-and-knees as you are starting to turn over is the result of not supporting your hands-and-knees landing and the start of the turnover with straight arms. To correct, review Step 2.

B. Insufficient turnover is most likely the result of not forcefully completing the leg-straightening, pointed-toe push-away that should be the principle rotational force in the stunt. To correct, review Steps 2 and 3 with this in mind.

C. Turning over crooked instead of straight down the middle is the most serious likely error and the hardest to correct. The underlying cause of the crooked turnover is fear. It is a kind of flinching action. The physical cause of crookedness may be a turning of the head to one side, a body bend that is not straight, or an uneven push away with the hands. Usually the best cure is to review Step 2 until all crookedness disappears and then progress slowly through Steps 3-5. Whenever crookedness reappears, back up one step. Patience is necessary.

Stunt No. 25—KNEE TURNPIKE
(Knee Drop, Forward Turnover Piked, to Sit)

DESCRIPTION OF ACTION. The first move after rather low preliminary bounces is a drop to a knee landing as in Stunt No. 6. The arms are circled through on the knee landing in order to enhance the lift. As you are leaving the bed again from the knee position, you must forcefully straighten the knees, pressing against the bed with the topside of the toes of the pointed foot (Fig. 25a). This knee-straightening is accompanied and followed by the spread of the arms sideward, the bending forward at the waist into the piked position, and the ducking of your head, pressing your chin against your chest (Figs. 25b and 25c). The

a) After landing in an erect kneeling position, the body has started to bend forward into the turnover. The straightening legs are assisting.

b) Getting into the piked position for continuing forward rotation.

c) With the forward turnover more than half-finished. The body will unbend to the sit and bounce to a stand.

Fig. 25. Knee turnpike.

piked turnover position is held until you are almost ready to land again. Before landing, you drop the hands to the sit-support position and straighten somewhat at the waist. The backward-leaning sit landing is followed by a rebound to a standing position.

STEPS IN LEARNING

1. The same background suggested under Step 1 for Stunt No. 24 is desirable for the Knee Turnpike. In addition, the knee drop and some combinations using the knee landing should have been practiced.

2. If you have not learned Stunt No. 24, you must begin this stunt by going through Steps 2-5 outlined for that stunt.

3. In a kneeling erect position, start bouncing up and down using the circling arm action to help you bounce. When ready, and as you are getting the lift from the bed on one of your bounces, start the knee-straightening pointed-toe press-away, spread your arms, bend at the waist and duck your head. Hold the position, especially the straight knees, until you land on the back or over toward the sit landing.

4. When you are efficient and confident on Step 3, you can substitute a low knee drop for the knee bounce. With the added height you can probably get over to the sit landing.

CORRECTION OF ERRORS

A. The knee landing can be the focal point of one or more errors. Letting the hips be forward of the body line when landing in the kneeling position can result in a wrenched back. Kneeling in a sitting heels position gives a very poor lift. Kneeling in a grossly forward-leaning position results in a dangerous forward travel and may even result in your head being bumped on the bed while you are turning over. The remedy for each of these errors is more practice and more success on the plain knee drop and easy combinations using the knee landing.

B. Starting the forward bending and ducking action before getting the lift from the knee landing well started will result in a backward traveling turnover or a very low turnover.

C. The cause of failure to get good rotation off the knees can often be traced to the failure to straighten the knees and press with the toes when leaving the knee landing.

D. Bent knees while turning over or when landing is not only bad form but it can be a danger. Your straight knees cannot hit you in the face; bent knees can.

E. For a cure for a crooked turnover, see Correction C under Stunt No. 24.

Stunt No. 26—TURNPIKE (From Feet, Forward Turnover Piked, to Sit)

DESCRIPTION OF ACTION. After the preliminary bounces, on the take-off for the turnpike you start bending forward at the waist by moving your hips backward and dropping your chest and shoulders forward (Fig. 26a). The legs follow through with their complete straightening, driving action to a pointed foot as you leave the bed on your way up. Your arms swing out of their take-off circle into the spread position for the turnover. As you are approaching the peak of the lift, you should duck your head and increase your bend at the waist to slightly speed up rotation (Fig. 26b). During the descent you should open up somewhat from the tight pike to a more open pike and drop the hands in preparation for the landing (Fig. 26c). The landing is in a backward-leaning sit position and leads to a rebound to a stand-up finish. There should be little or no forward travel during the entire stunt. The hips should land at about the spot where the feet were last in contact with the bed.

STEPS IN LEARNING

1. The minimum preparation for the turnpike would include controlled bounces, sit drops, piked front drops, and either knee turnpikes or hands-and-knees turnpikes (Stunts Nos. 24 or 25).

2. In a standing position on the floor, bend forward at the waist noticing how the hips have to move backward in order to keep the center of balance over the feet. Now do several of these forward bends, putting the arms out to the side and bending the head down so you are looking at your own middle.

3. Again in a standing position on the floor or on the trampoline, go through a series of arm circles as you imitate the bouncing action by doing a little knee-bending and straightening without leaving the surface on which you are standing. On one of these imitation take-offs, take your arm spread, forward bend at the waist, and head ducking in imitation of the turnover described above.

4. Using a moderate bounce, try the turnover from the feet take-off being sure that you keep your knees straight while turning over so that, as you land, you will not hit your face against your knees. Turning over not far enough is a preferable error to make than turning over too far, so take it somewhat easy on the first tries. Of course, it is very important that you get over at least as far as your back, so don't take it too easy.

CORRECTION OF ERRORS

A. Keeping the tight pike all the way to the landing results in a forward-bent sit landing which is a poor rebounding position and, if extreme, may be very uncomfortable as well. Practice the opening action even if it leaves you a little short of rotation

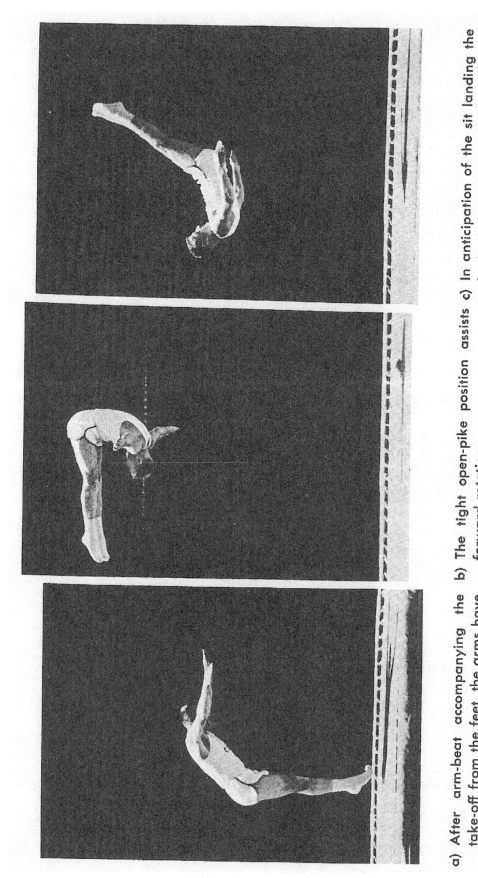

a) After arm-beat accompanying the take-off from the feet, the arms have stopped and the body bend has started.

b) The tight open-pike position assists forward rotation.

c) In anticipation of the sit landing the body has been straightened somewhat. A stand-up finish will follow the sit.

Fig. 26. Turnpike.

the first few times.

B. Traveling forward on the turnover beyond a few inches is a bad tendency and should be corrected before it gets worse and before it carries over into the somersault itself. Correct it by moving the hips backwards as you bend forward. Review Steps 2 and 3 with this in mind. Also, doing spotting (no forward travel) front drops may be a helpful corrective procedure.

C. Correction for overturning or under turning the landing involves correction of the timing and the force of the forward bend. Bending too forcefully or too early will give too much rotation and overturn the landing. Bending too gently or too late will result in too little rotation and an under turned landing. Experimentation with these two factors will help you to learn the best timing and optimum force.

D. If a crookedness or twisting action develops in the stunt, go immediately back to the very beginning turnover exercises to straighten it out.

Stunt No. 27—HANDS-AND-KNEES TURNTUCK
(Hands-and-Knees Drop, Forward Turnover Tucked, to Sit Drop)

DESCRIPTION OF ACTION. From the hands-and-knees landing, you rebound into the air, pressing down with the knee-straightening, pointed-foot action, as in the piked turnovers (Fig. 27a). You, of course, bend at the waist and duck the head also, as in the turnpikes. Here, however, there is one difference. Since you are going to use a tuck position during part of your rotation, thereby speeding up your turnover, you must allow for that by bending a little easier at first and ducking the head later. When you are off the bed in your piked position and at about the top of your flight, you quickly duck your head, bend the knees, grasp the shins, and, pull (Fig. 27b). This tuck position is held only very briefly and is followed by a kick-out from the tuck into the backward-leaning sit landing position (Fig. 27c). The sit landing is followed by the bounce to a stand.

STEPS IN LEARNING

1. Stunt No. 24 (and its prerequisites) should be considered as a necessary preliminary to this stunt. Experience with the tuck position can be gained from the tuck jump under Stunt NO.3.

2. Lie on your back on the trampoline with your knees bent as much as possible and drawn up to your chest and with your hands grasping and pulling on your shins, midway between your knees and ankles. In the tuck position, have your head tucked down against your chest and leave your knees far enough apart to leave a space for your head in between them. Now open out by releasing your hands, straightening your knees, and lifting your head. Come to the backward-leaning sit position on the bed. Repeat this several times to get the feel of this opening action so that you will be

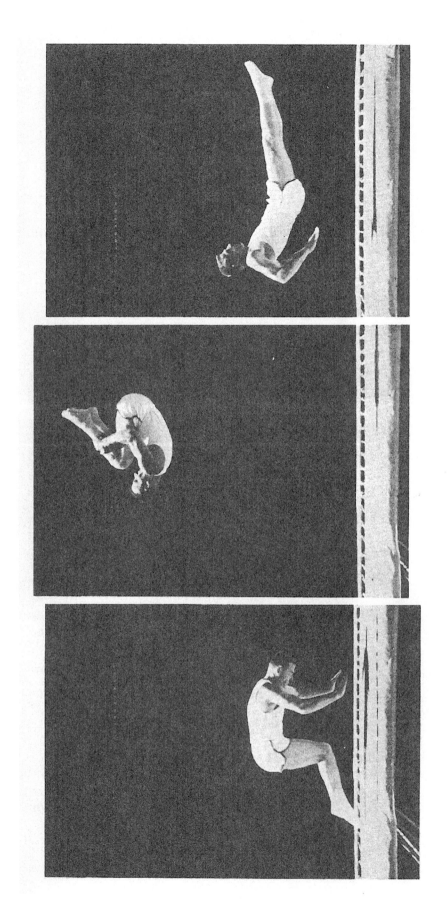

a) Leaving the hands-and-knees landing. b) Turning forward in the tuck position. c) With knees straightened and body position opened ready for sit landing.

Fig. 27. Hands-and-knees turntuck.

able to use it in mid-air.

3. Now from a lowish hands-and-knees drop, go into your turnover as if you were going to do a rather slow pike turnover with head up; then in mid-air, duck your head and change to the tuck position briefly. Open out before you hit. It is important to have your knees apart in case you should hit the bed before you remember to open out. This will protect your face from the possibility of hitting your knee.

4. Add a little more height as you gain more experience, but only modest height is suggested for this stunt, even in its finished form.

5. Use the same progression substituting knee drop for hands-and-knees drop for another variety of turn tuck.

CORRECTION OF ERRORS

A. Overturning can be corrected by delaying the body bend and the head ducking and by abbreviating the tuck.

B. Under turning is usually the result of not using the toe press (knee straightening) to get the hips up after the hands-and-knees take-off.

C. A tight tuck is important as a preparation for more advanced turnovers. A loose or sloppy tuck may be partly due to too much rotation which makes a tight tuck impossible to do without overturning the landing. Correct for overturning as in Correction A, above.

D. Crookedness of turnover may show up in this stunt, even if it has been avoided or overcome in other turnovers. Correct as suggested in Correction C under Stunt No. 24.

Stunt No. 28-TURNTUCK (From Feet, Tucked Turnover, to Sit Drop)

DESCRIPTION OF ACTION. From the regular arm-circling controlled bounce series, the take-off lift is begun as in each of the preliminary bounces with the leg drive and arm lift. As in the turnpike (Stunt No. 26), you begin bending at the waist by shifting the hips backward and the shoulders forward as you leave the bed (Fig. 28a). As compared to the turnpike, however, the forward bend is less forceful and the head ducking is delayed. At the peak of the jump the head is ducked, the body is bent more, the knees are doubled up and the hands are placed on the shins in a tuck position (Fig. 28b). The tuck is held briefly (during about 90 degrees of rotation), then released so that your legs can straighten, your angle at the waist can increase, and you can drop your hands back ready for the landing (Fig. 28c). The landing is a backward-leaning sit landing and is followed by a rebound to a stand. The forward travel in this stunt should be kept to a minimum.

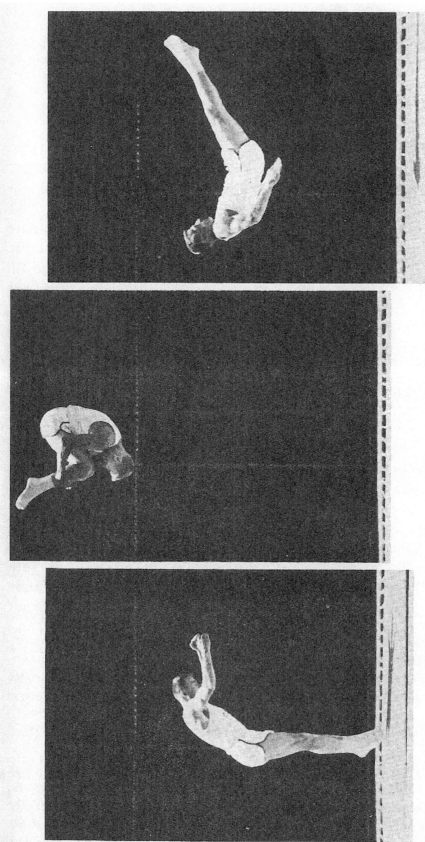

a) Starting the forward turnover from the feet take-off. Compared to Fig. 26a, notice body is less bent and arms are less straight.

b) After a tight tuck partial turnover, the tuck is beginning to loosen for the opening action.

c) With the opening complete ready for the sit landing.

Fig. 28. Turntuck.

STEPS IN LEARNING

1. If Stunts No. 26 and 27 (and all their prerequisites) have been well-learned, you are ready to proceed with the turn tuck from feet.

2. It may be helpful before trying the whole stunt to do a few under-turned turnpikes from the feet. In other words, you can bend a little less and keep the head up a little longer but maintain the straight-knee position until you land in something like a straight-knee back-drop position or between that and a sit. This should be done at a low or moderate height.

3. When trying the complete stunt the first few times, use the same low height and slowish start as in Step 2, but add the brief tuck after the leg drive, opening quickly again. Keep the knees apart in the tuck so that, if you land before you can get untucked, you won't bash your face against your knees.

CORRECTION OF ERRORS

A. Traveling forward more than a foot or two is an error which can be corrected by practicing some backward jumping with forward bending.

B. Tucking too soon results in a kind of knee-buckling action on the take-off which kills some of your height and some of your turnover, too. The feet should leave the bed with knees straight. To correct, think of this as a straight knee turnover (piked) with a brief tuck in the middle of it.

C. The corrections for loose tuck, crooked turnover, overturning, and underturning are substantially the same as for Stunt No. 27. Refer back to them if you find yourself in need of such corrections.

Stunt No. 29—TUCKED FORWARD SOMERSAULT
(From Feet, Tucked Forward Turnover, to Feet)

DESCRIPTION OF ACTION. The take-off action for the forward somersault should include the same arm action which you have learned for the controlled bounce. As you are taking your lift from the bed, your arms are swinging forward and upward and you are starting a slight forward bend at the waist (Fig. 29a). As you move toward the height of the lift, you increase the bend at the waist somewhat and slow down the arm lift to a stop (Fig. 29b). At about the top of the flight you suddenly duck your head, bend sharply at the waist and knees, and take hold of the shins with the hands (Fig. 29c). This tucked position then speeds up the rotation you have started with your early forward bending. You hold the tuck for about 90 degrees of rotation or a little more before you open (Fig. 29d). The first opening action is a partial straightening of the knees and a partial opening at the waist (Fig. 29e). In this partly straightened position, you first

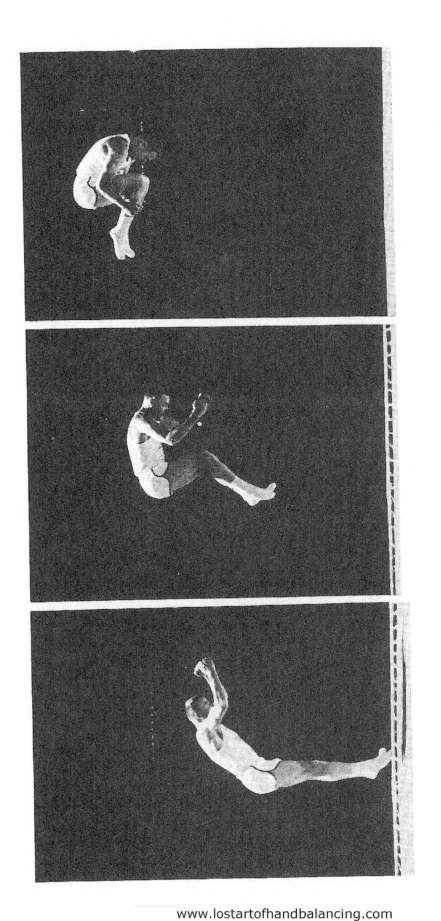

a) Just after take-off. The arms have b) With the leg drive completed, the c) Near the height of the bounce; the swung upward to this position and knees bend and the tucking starts. tuck is established; the arms are are now ready for the shins to come pulling. up to meet them.

Fig. 29. Tucked forward somersault.

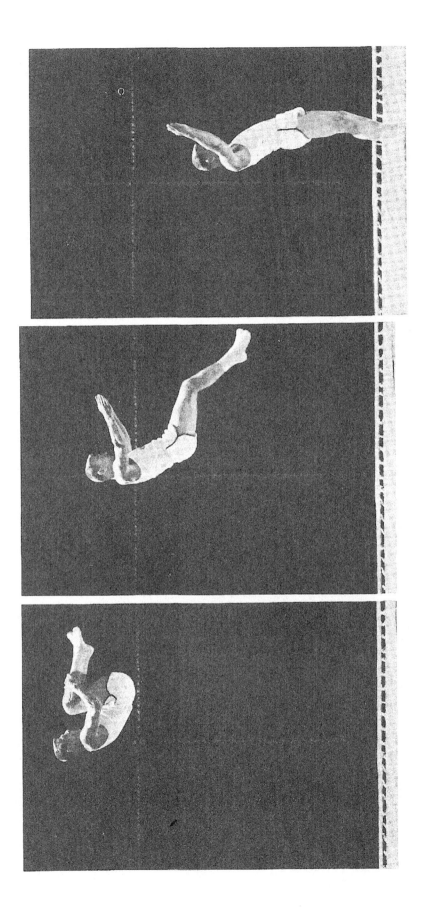

d) The turnover almost completed. The release of the tuck is imminent.

e) The opening action has slowed the spin. Eyes have located the bed.

f) The stand-up landing. A little less body-arch would be better.

Fig. 29. Continued.

locate the bed with your eyes, looking forward and downward past your opening legs. With practice, the information you acquire by sight at this point automatically enables you to determine how fast or how slowly the remainder of your opening should be to help stop rotation or continue it. You see how far you still have to drop and how much you need to rotate to land in a well-balanced stand-up or rebound landing (Fig. 29f). Ideally you continue the opening action smoothly and either get your arms in position for the circular sweep which accompanies your landing if you are going to "swing" right into another bounce or stunt, or get your arms into a forward-upward balance position if you are going to use a knee-break stop.

STEPS IN LEARNING

1. Stunts Nos. 24, 25, 26, 27, and 28 are essentially preparation stunts for this forward somersault. These stunts and their prerequisites should be well learned before trying the feet-to-feet turnover.

2. Using the knee turn tuck or hands-and-knees turntuck to sit as the starting point, begin increasing the rotation gradually by taking a little more forceful toe press, bending forward somewhat earlier, tucking more tightly and longer, and even by using a little more height. At first try to hit the heels before the seat on a sit landing. Next, try to open the legs out only about three-fourths of the way and hit on the soles of the feet before landing on the seat. Add some more rotation so that you are able to maintain a momentary support on the feet before bouncing to the seat or back or some other unpredictable position. Two admonitions are important here. Don't hold the tuck, or even most of the tuck, until you land. Always be opening. Second, don't be driving your knees forcefully straight at the time your feet hit on the bed as this will send you flying backward and maybe off the bed. The landing after about a three-quarter opening should be made with some give in the knees to prevent an uncontrolled rebound.

3. If you are efficient on your knees or hands-and-knees take-offs, you will be able to complete your somersault to a stand from one of these take-offs by increasing the forces applied in Step 2 until the time you land on your feet and stay there. The advantage of learning it from one or both of these two take-offs before trying it from the feet is that it gives you an opportunity to make and correct your mistakes at a lower and safer height.

4. After you have become experienced with the feet landings, or near-to-standing landings, by practicing Steps 2 and 3, you should review the turn tuck from feet to seat. Begin to turn it over a little bit farther each successive time until you are able to hit the soles of your feet first before sitting and then finally are able to stay on your feet without falling down. It will take many, many repetitions before you are sure of yourself.

CORRECTION OF ERRORS

A. The most common error is the tendency to try to take a shortcut to learning. The chances of having a good somersault and of avoiding even a minor injury are so much greater if you will go through the suggested preparatory stunts and learning procedure, doing each of them carefully and thoroughly.

B. Letting the head follow the spin (staying back instead of forward) is an error that makes control most difficult. Your eyes should stay open all the way. You will not see anything helpful while in the tuck, but you want to be ready to see as soon as possible while opening. You should spot (i.e., look) forward and downward until near the top when you duck and tuck. As you open, your eyes should be seeking the same spot on the trampoline that was their point of focus before ducking.

C. Failure to turn over far enough to come to a stand-up landing is usually due to an incomplete leg drive before tucking or to an insufficient early forward bend at the waist while taking the lift. To correct either of these tendencies it is helpful to think of driving the hips up behind as in a pike turnover before converting to a tuck position.

D. A tendency to bounce off the trampoline after landing, or dangerously near to the edge, is due to either an underturning or overturning of the somersault. In learning through many repetitions to be more accurate in controlling the amount of rotation, it is wise to make your landings with a little knee-break stop (Stunt No.2) to prevent a rebound which might be traveling dangerously forward or backward.

E. To correct crookedness, it is often necessary to go all the way back to the beginning of the forward turnover group and patiently work your way up again.

Stunt No. 30—PIKED FORWARD SOMERSAULT
(From Feet, Piked Forward Turnover, to Feet)

DESCRIPTION OF ACTION. The take-off is from a fairly high series of controlled bounces, using a good arm circle to add to the force exercised against the bed. As you are being lifted into the air you bend very sharply at the waist, ducking your head forcefully (Fig. 30a), grasping your legs behind the knees and pulling in with the strength of your bending arms (Fig. 30b). After holding this closed pike position briefly, you open at the waist without letting your knees bend, straightening your body ready for the landing (Fig. 30c). Your eyes should seek out the surface of the bed as you are opening in order to give you information which will help you determine whether you need to open faster or slower to land in good balance.

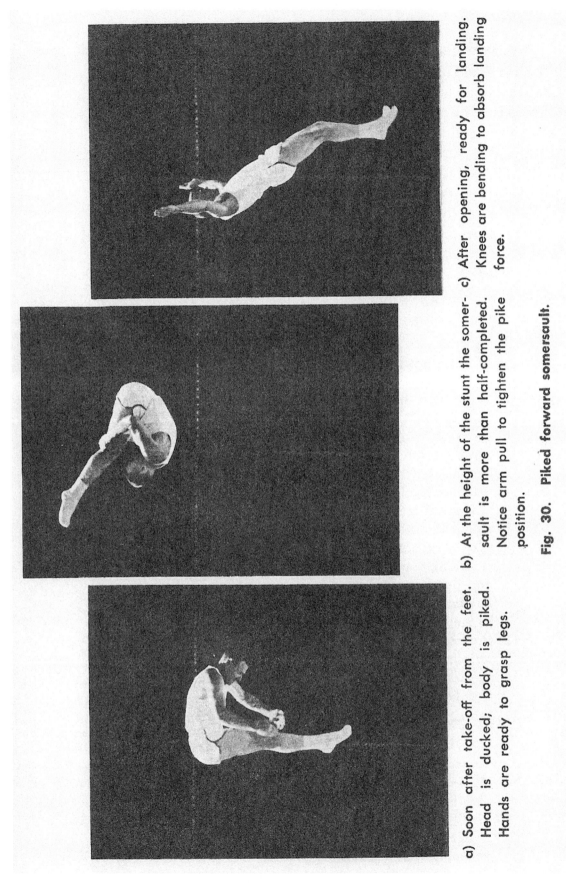

a) Soon after take-off from the feet. Head is ducked; body is piked. Hands are ready to grasp legs.

b) At the height of the stunt the somersault is more than half-completed. Notice arm pull to tighten the pike position.

c) After opening, ready for landing. Knees are bending to absorb landing force.

Fig. 30. Piked forward somersault.

STEPS IN LEARNING

1. You need to have learned to do the tucked forward somersault and, of course, the stunts that are prerequisite to it before undertaking the piked somersault.

2. Sit on the trampoline or on the floor and take hold of the backs of your knees, slipping your palms under your legs from the outside. Keep your knees straight as you bend your arms bringing the face as near the shins as you can. This is the tight pike position that you need to get into during part of your turnover.

3. From a *very small* bounce do a fast turnpike to sit (Stunt No. 26); but instead of putting your arms out sideward, use the hands-under-the-knees grasp. Release the tight pike in time for a regular sit landing with hands on the bed behind the hips.

4. From a medium high bounce take the same fast start and tight pike as in Step 3, hold the pike a little longer, and then open up sharply to a stand. Use the knee-break stop as you land for the first few tries at least.

CORRECTION OF ERRORS

A. Letting the knees bend during the turnover spoils the pike form. To keep them straight, review Steps 2 and 3 in the learning procedure.

B. A slow turnover, leaving no time for straightening out before landing, is usually a result of a forward bend that is too late or too slow moving. Practice Step 3 as low and fast as you can. Complete the forward bend by pulling in with bent arms.

C. Overturning the landing is most often the result of not opening soon enough or completely enough. Keeping your eyes open and looking for the bed about 2 yards ahead of the feet will also help you control the landing.

Stunt No. 31-FORWARD DIVE TO BACK DROP

DESCRIPTION OF ACTION. This is a forward turnover stunt with even less forward turnover than the turnovers to sit landings. It is placed here in the sequence of stunts because both experience and confidence are needed to do it safely. The take-off from a moderate bounce is with a forward bend at the waist, as in the beginning of a turnpike to sit (Fig. 31a). The head is not ducked as the peak is reached, but remains in a position which enables you to continue to watch the bed as you turn over. As you pass the peak and start down you unbend at the waist as much as is necessary to keep from losing sight of your landing spot (Fig. 31b). When near the mat and descending inverted vertically you duck your head, bend more at the waist, and drop onto your back as in the straight-knee back drop (Fig. 31c). The recovery to the feet is also the same as in that stunt.

a) Turning forward without ducking the head.

b) Body straightened, still watching the bed. Heading for apparent disaster.

c) With head ducked, body bent and knees straight, safe back landing is made. A subsequent opening action will facilitate recovery to a stand.

Fig. 31. Forward dive to back drop.

STEPS IN LEARNING

1. Learning the straight-knee back drop plus the turnpike to sit and all its prerequisites are necessary before undertaking to learn the forward dive to back drop.

2. Begin with the turnovers from knees and from hands-and-knees, trying to keep the head up until the last moment and then ducking under just far enough to land on the back.

3. From a low bounce, try the same technique of watching the mat as long as possible from a feet take-off, starting like the turnpike and ducking under to the back.

4. To get the feel of the action of opening and then ducking under, which makes the dive better controlled and more spectacular, the handstand may be helpful. With hands and feet on the bed and head up (pyramid position), bounce with the feet a couple of times (hands stay on the bed) and open to a handstand on the bed. Ride the handstand over past balance, then pick up the hands, duck the head, and bend at the waist to land on the back.

5. Proceed as in Step 3, but bend more forcefully at first so that it is necessary to open out as in Step 4 toward a handstand position above the bed in order to prevent overturn. Duck under easily and late to the back and bounce to the feet.

CORRECTION OF ERRORS

A. The most common error is ducking too soon and especially too far under, thus passing by the correct landing angle before dropping to the, bed. Correcting this fault must be done gradually and cautiously. It is obviously a better error than not ducking enough or soon enough.

B. Letting the knees collapse as you land on your back is not only a little dangerous as it may put your knees in your face, but it also kills the rebound. Emphasize straight knees on your build-up stunts.

C. Holding a steady pike instead of opening in preparation for the final duck under is a less satisfactory and less spectacular form. A stronger or earlier forward bend at the beginning will make the opening possible.

Stunt No. 32- TUCKED FORWARD ONE-AND-ONE-QUARTER SOMERSAULT

DESCRIPTION OF ACTION. The take-off is almost identical to that for the tucked forward somersault (Stunt No. 29). You will need more rotation to complete this stunt so you may bend a little sharper at the waist to bring this about. You change into your head-down, tucked position at the top of the flight as in the tucked somersault to feet (Fig. 32a) but do not release again so

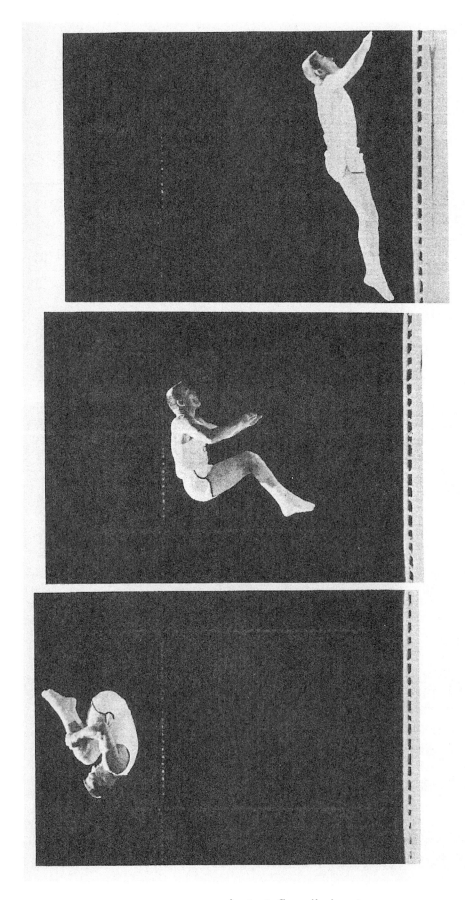

a) In tight tuck position after three-quarters forward turnover. b) Well past the single somersault rotation, the opening action begins. c) With the opening complete ready for the front landing. Rebound to the feet will follow.

Fig. 32. Tucked forward one-and-one-quarter somersault.

soon. You can let the tuck loosen up a little as you pass the full somersault position (Fig. 32b). The loosened position gives you a chance to see how near the bed you are and how far you have yet to turn so that you can judge how fast to complete your opening to make a front drop landing (Fig. 32c). From the front drop you rebound to your feet by pushing and bending as you previously have learned to do.

STEPS IN LEARNING

1. The tucked forward somersault (Stunt No. 29) should be well-learned along with its prerequisite stunts and the front drop should be thoroughly reviewed before starting to learn the one-and-one-quarter forward somersault.

2. Substitute a tuck for the pike in such stunts as the front drop, the sit drop to front drop, and back drop to front drop, and do several of each.

3. Do your tucked forward somersault, overturning it a little bit to land on your feet in a bent-forward-at-the-waist position with the hands coming to the bed soon after the feet.

4. The tucked forward somersault with enough overturn to land on the hands-and-knees may be a good step in the learning progression from a psychological point of view.

5. You may not want to do more than one or two of the hands-and-knees landings or you may want to skip it altogether because you will find the front landing is actually easier.

CORRECTION OF ERRORS

A. It is a mistake to differ much from the technique you use for the forward somersault to feet. If you start to spin much earlier or harder, you will overspin your landing. The main difference between the one and one-quarter and the one is in holding the tuck a little longer.

B. To open all the way at once to the straight position makes it very likely that you will not consistently hit flat, as you want to. The opening should be part way at first to a semi-tuck or a pike position; then, after you see where you are, the rest of the straightening takes place.

Stunt No. 33-BALL-OUT FORWARD SOMERSAULT TO SIT
(Forward Somersault from Back Drop to Sit Drop)

DESCRIPTION OF ACTION. Well behind the center of the trampoline bed, after a series of preliminary bounces, drop to a back landing as you have learned to do for the kick-out back drop (Stunt No.9). Just as you make contact with the bed, kick out forward and upward at about a 45-degree angle by extending the legs and unbending some at the waist (Fig. 33a). Your kick-out is

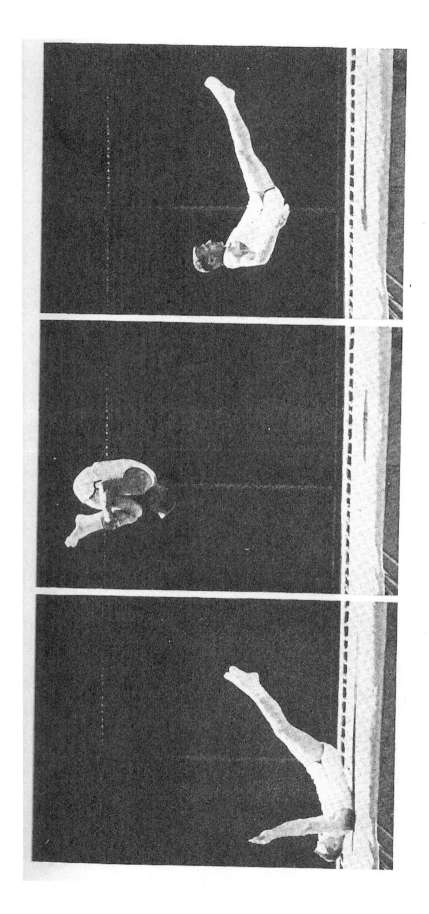

a) This kick-out follows the doubled-up b) After the kick-out. Forward rotation c) Kick out to sit landing, then bounce
drop to the back.   is aided by the tight tuck.   to feet.

Fig. 33. Ball-out forward somersault to sit.

followed immediately by ducking your head and doubling up again into a hands-on-shins tuck (Fig. 33b). The tuck is held until you have turned all the way over, past the back-toward-the-bed position in the air. Open out of the tuck to a straight-knees, pointed-feet, backward-leaning sit landing (Fig. 33c). Bounce from the sit landing to a standing finish.

STEPS IN LEARNING

1. The kick-out back drop, the back drop to front drop, the forward dive to back drop, and the turn tuck to sit landing are the essential background stunts involved here. These four, especially, and many other stunts previously described should be learned before undertaking this ball-out somersault from the back landing.

2. Do a back drop and turn forward as if going to a front drop, but hold the piked position and land on the hands and feet (pyramid position). After landing, roll immediately over onto your back and seat.

3. After several repetitions of Step 2, make the kick-out at a slightly lower angle and with a little more force and try to duck under onto the back before landing, as in the forward dive to back drop (Stunt No. 31).

4. When you can accomplish Step 3 with ease, you will have the confidence to try for the tucked turnover to seat by ducking your head right after your kick-out and doubling up into a tuck. Be sure to kick out of the tuck before landing.

CORRECTION OF ERRORS

A. Inability to get enough turnover to come easily to your sit landing is generally due to the poor timing of your kick-out. If you kick a little too late, the lift is decreased considerably. Kicking too straight up would also cut down on rotation, as would failure to make a sufficiently complete or snappy enough kick-out before going into the tuck. To correct these faults, go back to the easier stunts such as the back drop and the back drop to front drop and concentrate on over-correcting your error.

B. This stunt travels forward quite a bit at best. To avoid going off the bed, don't start in the middle or forepart of the bed, and don't kick forward at a very low angle.

ADDITIONAL FORWARD SOMERSAULT STUNTS LISTED

There are many other forward somersault stunts which you can undertake after you have had the experience of learning the ones described and pictured in this chapter. To learn them readily and safely you must develop for yourself a learning progression and put to use the basic applicable information from the foregoing pages. A list of some of these additional somersault stunts follows:

1. Forward somersault piked from hands-and-knees to feet

2. Forward somersault piked from knees to feet

3. Forward somersault from knees or hands-and-knees to hands-and-knees or front landing

4. Forward dive to back, forward turnover to back, bounce to feet (dive to dive or porpoise)

5. Forward somersault one and one-quarter from back drop to feet (ball-out somersault)

6. Forward somersault to feet from dive to back (dive to ball-out somersault)

7. Forward somersault with an open pike (arms out to side instead of under the legs)

8. One-and-a-quarter forward somersault piked from feet to front drop

9. From the landing of one forward somersault, take-off immediately to a second forward somersault (swing time forward somersaults)

10. Forward somersault one-and-a-half(duck under onto back)

6

Advanced
Knick-Knacks

In this chapter we explore the performance techniques, the learning procedures, and the methods of preventing and correcting errors for a few selected stunts from a group I have chosen to call advanced knick-knacks. At the end of the chapter there is a list of some additional stunts in the same category which will challenge your ability to transfer the skills and principles you have learned to new positions and combinations.

The two things which all of these stunts have in common are that they are difficult to learn and they do not depend on daring somersaults to give them the element of difficulty. Many of them are more difficult than somersaults, but at the same time less hazardous. If you can master them, you will have some stunts which put you a notch above your friends who do not have the diligence and patience to learn them.

At any rate, I strongly recommend that you use the learning of these stunts to postpone your venture into the backward somersaults until you have had more experience or until you can arrange to use a safety belt for learning. Even after you have begun belt work for the backward somersaults, you may have much practice time between your opportunities in the belt. This time can be used to review the previously learned stunts and also to learn some of the stunts in this chapter which you may have skipped in your anxiety to get to the backward somersaults.

These knick-knacks are not only challenging and intriguing in themselves, but many also contain elements which are identical to elements in the most advanced twisting somersaults. Learning these stunts in the relatively early part of your trampoline career will make it much easier to learn the really big somersault twisters when you get to them.

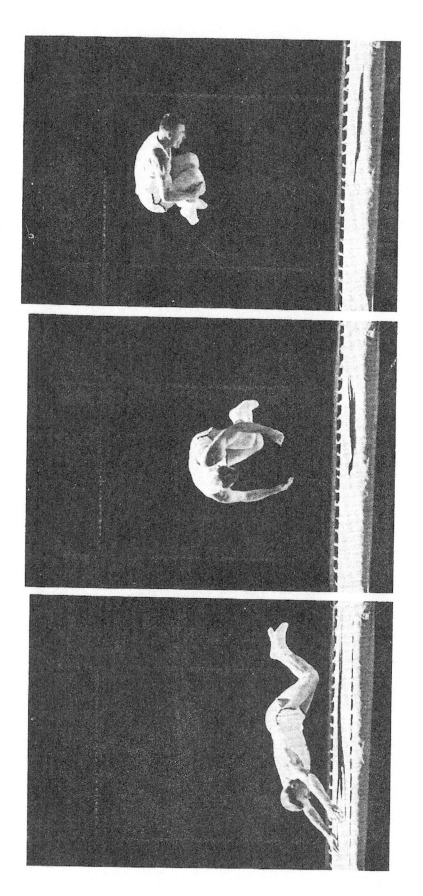

a) Starting the turn after the front b) One-quarter turn completed. Body c) After half a turn. Head pulling to landing. Notice the immediate dou- almost tucked. the left. Arms pulling on shins. bling-up action; notice the claw grip.

Fig. 34. Full turntable.

d) Three-quarters turn completed. Just   e) Almost around. Opening out of tuck.   f) The turn is completed. Ready for sec-
starting to release tuck.   ond front landing. Rebound to a
                                                                                   stand will finish the stunt.

Fig. 34.   Continued.

Stunt No. 34—THE FULL TURNTABLE
(Front Drop, Full Turn, Front Drop)

DESCRIPTION OF ACTION. You go into the air from your preliminary bounces into a slightly forward-tipping and slightly forward-bent position, without at the same time traveling forward. At the top of the lift, you increase the bend at the waist. Hold the semi-jackknife until you are near the bed with the hands and feet at about the same level, then open out to the front landing. This landing differs a little from the ordinary front landing in that the arms are on the bed in such a way as to exert lateral pressure to help you to get moving fast on your turn when you are leaving the bed. If the turn is to be to the left (as it is in the illustration), the arms are placed down to the left of their usual places. On a woven bed, putting the hands in a claw-like position also helps to get traction for a sideward push. As you are being lifted up by the bed (Fig. 34a), you begin immediately your turning movement by looking and turning your head extremely to the left against your left shoulder, pushing to the right with your hands and arms, and bending sideward (like an alligator turning a corner) at the waist. To amplify this turn, you pull yourself immediately into a close, hands-on-shins tuck position (Figs. 34b and 34c). Hold the tuck while you complete 360 degrees of turn (Figs. 34d and 34e). Release the tuck and open up to another front landing (Fig. 34f). Push down with the arms in order to bounce up to a stand.

STEPS IN LEARNING

1. The ability to do good front drops and half turntables is of course essential to being ready to try the full turntable. The tuck should have been learned by trying it at the height of the bounce as in Stunt No. 3 or by doing it in forward somersault stunts as in Chapter 5.

2. First of all, put some protective cover over bare elbows and knees. Now, on the trampoline bed, get down on your knees, sit down on your heels, put your chest down against the top of your thighs and your forearms on the bed beside your knees. This tightly tucked position is to be your landing position after the turn for the next two or three learning steps.

3. On your hands and knees, bounce up and down a few times. On one of your level bounces, change to the front landing. From the front landing, push sideways, bend sideways, turn the head sideways and double up into the position you learned for Step 2. Land facing the side of the trampoline just 90 degrees around from your original facing. Land in the tightly tucked position in which you were turning and which you have practiced for Step 2.

4. With a higher preliminary hands-and-knees bounce, and with a more forceful sideward push of the hands and turn of the head and a momentary grasping of your shins during the turn, you should be able to increase the amount of turn to a three-quarters turn (270

degrees) or more. Continue also to use the tight tuck landing position with the hands on the bed. Utilize the off-center arm position and claw grip on the front drop to increase the turning force you exert against the bed.

5. Substitute a low front drop from the feet for the front drop from hands-and-knees bounce in Step 4 and you will have enough height to do the complete 360-degree turn. When you are able to land in the tuck position facing the same direction as that in which you started the turn, then you are ready to try opening out of the tuck to the front landing at the end of the turn and bounce up to your feet.

CORRECTION OF ERRORS

A. There is a natural tendency to lift the leading shoulder up when starting the turn. This results in a sideward rolling or twisting and makes it impossible to have a level landing. In order to keep the front side squarely towards the bed all the way, it is necessary to make a special effort to keep the leading shoulder (left if you are turning to the left) down. Keep the head down beside the shoulder and think of that leading shoulder as if it were the low wing of an airplane on a bank turn.

B. Failure to double up into a tight tuck cuts down on your speed of turn. Grasping the shins and pulling in gives a faster and more spectacular spin than even the tightest tuck without grasping the shins. To correct the loose tuck habit, go back to learning Step 4, paying special attention to the tuck.

C. The sluggish turn or inability to get around the full 360 degrees, even though tucking properly, is not uncommon. There are several avenues of correction for this. Each should be tried until a successful combination is attained. First, make the turning-force movements sudden, forceful, and explosive. This means the head turn, the sideward push and the sideward bend must be done early and snappily. Second, you may need to place your hands more to the left (assuming a left turn) on the front landing. Some have success only by reaching the left arm almost straight out sideward and the right hand across to the left of the head. Third, you may need to get a finger of one or both hands between the webbings to get a real grip to pull and push against. In using the latter technique, be sure to remove the finger quickly or you may harm not only the spin but the finger as well.

Stunt No. 35—CORKSCREW
(Back Drop, One and One-Half Twist, Back Drop)

DESCRIPTION OF ACTION. From a medium high series of bounces, take off as for another bounce except tip back slightly as you leave the bed. After your feet have left the bed, start bending your knees and drawing them up to your chest, keeping your feet pointed and your sight still forward and downward. You land on

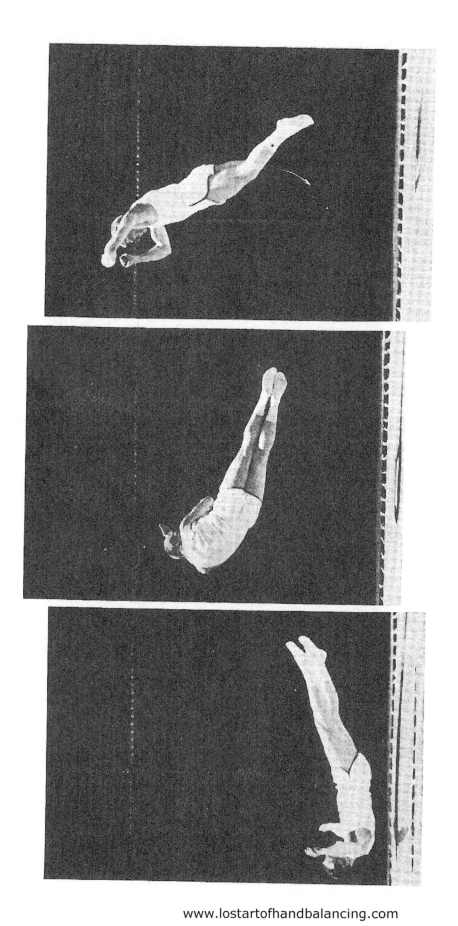

a) From the back landing the kick-out is
almost straight ahead.

b) The cross-body arm action has started
the twist as the body rotates forward.

c) Half a twist is complete before body
reaches vertical.

Fig. 35.   Corkscrew.

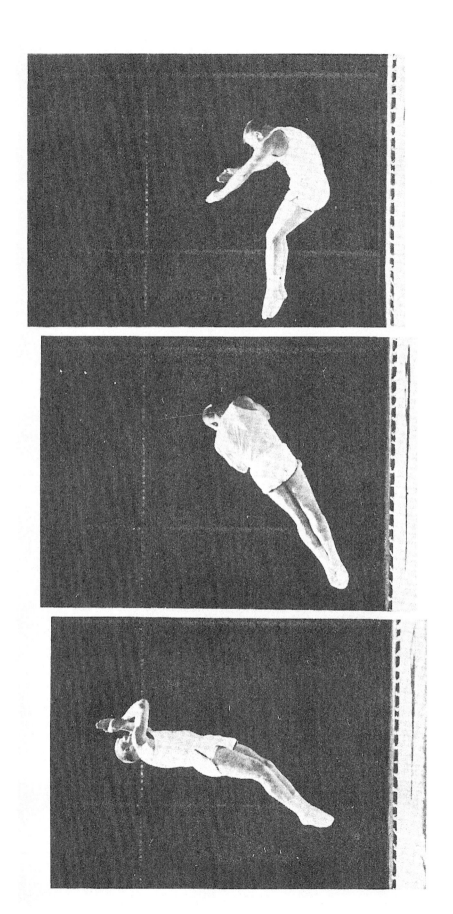

d) Almost a full twist now, with body rotated past the vertical.

e) With only a little way to drop, one-and-a-quarter twists are completed.

f) The twist finished ready for the back landing.

Fig. 35. Continued.

your back near the point where your feet left the bed as in the kick-out back drop (Stunt No. 9). The kick-out follows immediately after making the first contact on the bed with the back. The direction of the kick should be a little above the horizontal. You straighten your body as soon as possible and spread your arms (Fig. 35a). As soon as you are in the air with arms wide, body fairly straight and rotating forward as if your objective were to end up in a front drop, you very quickly throw your right arm across your chest (Fig. 35b), pull the left arm in against your chest (or let one or both arms go overhead), turn your head as far to the left as possible and keep straight while you spin (Figs. 35c and 35d). As you are completing one and one-half twists (Fig. 35e) you are continuing to rotate forward as in the cradle (Stunt No 23). The next landing therefore is on the back facing opposite to your previous landing with the body bent at the waist as in the straight-knee back drop (Fig. 35f). From this landing, you bounce to your feet with the straight-knee back drop recovery action. If you wish to have a strong lift from this final back drop as if, for instance, you are going to do another corkscrew from your back without returning to your feet, you should use the bent-knee, kick-out style of landing instead of the straight-knee style described above.

STEPS IN LEARNING

1. As background for this stunt, you will need confident mastery of at least the controlled bounces, back drop, back drop to front drop; half twist to back drop, and late-twisting cradle.

2. Do a half twist to back drop (Stunt No. 14), but with a little less than the usual amount of forward tip and without bending at the waist for the landing. The landing will be a flat-back (body straight, legs straight, horizontal supine) landing.

3. With a similar beginning (as in Step 2), being sure your arms are wide and that you have started a little twist on the take-off, throw your arm across more vigorously, pull in tighter, hang on longer, and keep straight all the way. Complete a full twist then open your arms and come to a front landing. Don't start the strong twisting action right off the bed. Wait until you are in the air looking at the bed in front of you before you throw your arm and turn your head into the twist.

4. When you are repeatedly successful with Step 3, you can try the same full twist to front drop from the kick-out back drop. Build up to it by first doing a few back drops to front drops, trying to keep as straight at the waist as you can between the back landing and the front landing. Next, try the late-twisting cradle with straight body to flat-back landing (similar to Step 2 above). Then you are ready to throw the twist a little sooner and a little harder and keep wrapped up longer to get the full twist to front drop from the back drop. As in Step 3, you can start to twist a little right off the bed, but wait until you are completely free of the bed turning forward toward a front drop

and with body straight before you turn your head and throw your arm for the fast twist.

5. After a few of these full twists from back drop to front drop, you should try to twist farther by continuing to turn the head and holding the wrap-up of the arms until you land. The landings will be at first on your side, then later on your flat-back; finally you will be able to get around all the way and then bend at the waist for the regular back drop landing.

CORRECTION OF ERRORS

A. The most common error on the corkscrew is the concentration of all effort on the twist to the neglect of the kick-out and forward rotation. Delaying the throw for the twist will help cure this tendency. As you get more accomplished at doing the completed stunt, you can let the twist come earlier without losing the rotation, but at first it is most helpful to sort of "see your way over the top" before turning your head and throwing your fast twist.

B. The other common error that prevents an effective performance is bending at the waist or at the knees when part way through the twist, thus slowing or stopping the twist. This is usually due to an anxiety to get in a protective landing position. Going back through the learning steps with the straight position emphasized and then trying for the flat-back landing in Step 5 will often quickly correct this error.

Stunt No. 36—CAT TWIST (Back Drop, Full Twist, Back Drop)

DESCRIPTION OF ACTION. After a few controlled bounces of medium height, and when you are mentally set, take the kind of lift that puts you into the kick-out back drop landing position (Stunt No. 9), but with just a little more of backward rotation. The kick-out is timed for maximum lift as in the plain kick-out back drop, but instead of kicking upward and a little forward the kick-out in this case needs to be nearly straight up, almost directly above the middle of your body. As you are starting the extension of the knees and hips in the kick-out action, you must at the same time start a corkscrew-like legs and hip twist (Fig. 36a) similar to that in the half twist from back drop (Stunt No. 18). As your body and legs straighten with a twisting stretch toward the ceiling or sky, you continue to watch your feet until you are well straightened and the twist is well underway. At this point you turn your head and shoulders to follow your hip twist, looking first around at the bed (Fig. 36b), then continuing on around to look again straight up (Fig. 36c). Thus the shoulders lead the way in the latter part of the twist after trailing in the early part. The landing is made by bending at the waist and at the knees to put yourself in the same kick-out back drop position which you were in just before you did the full twist. Another kick-out, this time forward and upward will give you a recovery to a stand-up finish. Either or both back drops can be

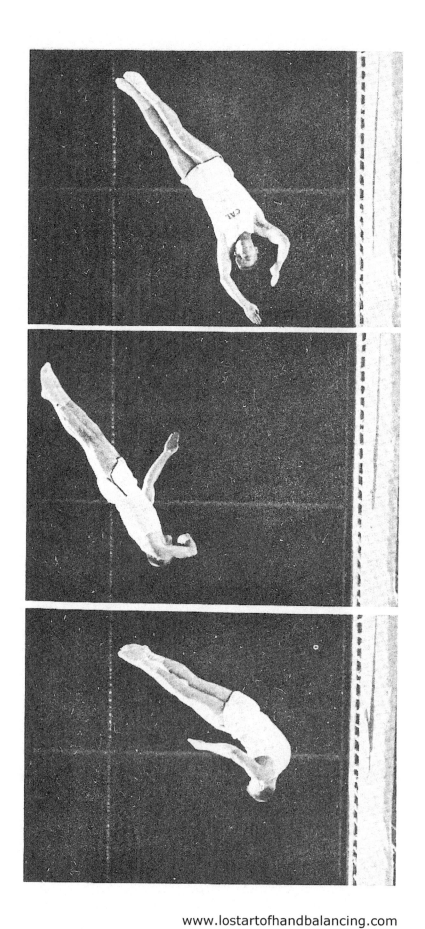

a) After the first back drop, the high-angle, twisting kick-out.

b) At the highest point, half twist complete.

c) Still twisting, coming in for the second back landing.

Fig. 36. Cat twist.

done in the straight-knee style, but the lift is less effective from the back and therefore the height of the stunt or of the rebound will be less.

STEPS IN LEARNING

1. Be sure that among the many stunts you have learned to do before you start on the cat twist are back drops and combinations of other stunts with back drops. Especially valuable for background would be the half twist from back drop and the early-twisting cradle.

2. Start from a position on your back on the trampoline bed with your bent legs pointing up. Bounce up and down on your back by extending your legs and bending them again. To keep on your back and not come up to a sit, it is necessary to kick straight up each time.

3. Take a small drop from feet to a kick-out style back landing, kick almost straight up without any twist, then land on the back again, and rebound to a stand. Increase the height of the drop on successive tries and increase the extent of the kick-out until you are able to do a complete stretch between back landings.

4. If you have rehearsed your hip-twisting kick-out action in the stunts suggested in Step 1 and have learned the vertical kick-out and stretch between back landings as explained in Step 3, you are ready to combine the near-vertical angle of kick-out with the twisting stretch and thereby make a good try at the cat twist itself. Your first try, using the drop from the feet to the back, should give you enough twist to get past the half twist and enable you to land on one shoulder. After a few more tries you should be getting around comfortably near the back landing. From here on, it's just a matter of patience and practice.

CORRECTION OF ERRORS

A. Kicking very far forward of vertical will result in something approaching a sit landing instead of a second back drop. Practice Step 3.

B. Rolling into the twist before getting a square take-off from the back will send the stunt off sideways. To correct, remember to watch your feet as you start the twisting extension and point them "up the center."

C. Inability to get all the way around on the twist may be a result of insufficient stretch with the twist or of insufficient twist with the stretch: get a maximum of both. Twist can be aided also by having a wide-arm position during the hip-twisting kick and wrapping the arms in tight as the shoulders twist.

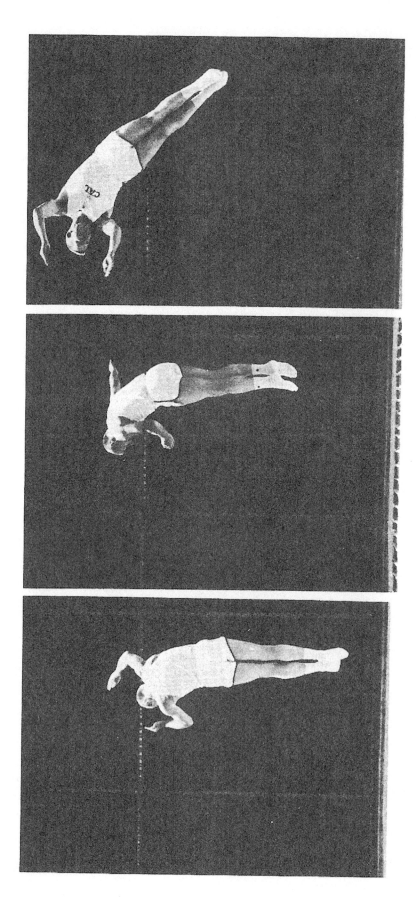

a) Just after the take-off from the feet. b) After half a twist. Arm ready for c) Three-quarters of a twist. Eyes still Look-around twist already started. cross-body swing. watching bed.

Fig. 37. Double twist to back drop.

d) One-and-one-quarter twist. Head has done almost a complete twist since previous picture.

e) One-and-three-quarters twist. Landing time is near, but body is still straight.

f) Double twist complete. Body bending for back landing. Rebound to a stand-up to follow.

Fig. 37. Continued.

Stunt No. 37—DOUBlE TWIST TO BACK DROP

DESCRIPTION OF ACTION. After a series of medium-high, controlled bounces, you take off with a backward tipping action by pulling the shoulders back and pushing the hips forward. As you are taking your lift, you simultaneously turn your trunk and head around to your left (or right), spreading your arms and keeping your body fairly straight (Fig. 38a). This puts you in the position early in your upward flight in which you are falling toward and looking at the part of the bed which was directly behind you when you started (Fig. 37b). From here, you speed up your twist greatly by throwing your right arm across your body (if you are twisting to the left), pulling both arms in close to the chest or overhead and turning your head strongly toward the direction of twist (Figs. 37c and 37d). You hold this wrapped-up, straight-body position until you have completed an additional one and one-half twists (Fig. 37e). To stop the twist, you open the arms out, and bend at the waist (Fig. 37f). The landing is the same as for the straight-knee back drop. From your back, you bounce to your feet.

STEPS IN LEARNING

1. You should at least be proficient at controlled bounces, sit drops, back drops, hands-and-knees drops, and front drops. It would be most helpful to have learned the half-twist to back drop (Stunt No. 16), the half-twist to front drop (Stunt No. 17) and the corkscrew (Stunt No. 36) before starting to learn the double twist to back drop.

2. From a low bounce, take off with a little backward tip, turn the head and shoulders immediately keeping the body straight. Take a quick look at the part of the bed which was behind you when you started, throw your arm across your chest easily, bend at the waist, and come to a sit landing facing your original direction. This is a full twist to a sit.

3. From a low bounce, take off with a little more backward tip than in Step 2, turn immediately to face the bed as in Step 2, then execute the twisting and landing movements you learned for the half twist to back drop (Stunt No. 16). This is a full twist to back drop.

4. Review or learn Step 2 of the learning procedure for the corkscrew (Stunt No. 36). This is a full twist to front drop.

5. Begin with the backward tip and quick-look-around half twist and finish by doing the full twist after the look-around. You land as in Step 4 in a front landing. This, then, is a one and one-half twist to front drop.

6. With a somewhat bigger starting bounce now, repeat Step 5; but instead of opening out to land on the front, continue to twist onto the back. The landings for these first tries may be best

done as flat-back landings. They can be developed into regular bent-body back landings by adding a little more backward rotation at the beginning of the stunt and by bending at the waist at the finish.

CORRECTION OF ERRORS

A. The most common cause of trouble in this stunt is the failure to keep your body straight while twisting. Practice each step of the learning procedure, concentrating on the elimination of the bends at the knees and waist and using the flat-back landing on Steps 3 and 6.

B. Lack of control and lack of twist can both be at least partially cured by the proper use of your head positions. Turn it early 180 degrees (half turn), look briefly at the bed, let it spin another 360 degrees (full turn), look at the bed again very briefly, then turn it another half turn to its final position.

C. Lack of twist may be due to failure to spread the arms on the first half twist, failure to "wrap up" forcefully during the final one and one-half twists, or failure to keep straight while twisting.

ADDITIONAL ADVANCED KNICK-KNACKS LISTED

1. Forward dive to back drop to corkscrew

2. Forward dive to back drop, forward turn with full twist to duck under (dive) to back drop

3. Back pullover with one and one-half twist to back drop

4. One and one-half and double turntables

5. One and one-half twisting swivel hips (swivel hips with additional

full twist)

6. Double twisting barrel roll (barrel roll with additional full twist)

7. Front drop double twist to front drop

8. Two and one-half twist to back drop (forward tip)

9. Back drop, double twist to back drop (cat twist with additional full twist)

10. Forward dive to back drop, two and one-half twists, to back drop (dive to corkscrew with extra full twist)

7

The Backward
Somersault Group

The backward somersault, commonly called the back flip, is in its essential form a complete turnover backwards, springing from the feet and landing again on the feet. Like the forward somersault, it has many variations of style and is done in multiples and fractions according to the amount of rotation involved. Backward turnovers are done from several different take-off positions also. Altogether the variety is considerable. I have selected seven of the more important backward somersault stunts to present in detail now. A few additional ones are listed at the end of this chapter. Some twisting backward somersaults are described in Chapter 8, and many backward somersaults of more advanced difficulty are mentioned in Chapter 9.

Backward somersaults are not more difficult to do than forward somersaults, but they are harder to learn and more treacherous in the learning. A combination of three reasons accounts for the problems involved in learning these stunts. First of all, there is no very good, safe, step-by-step, do-it-yourself progression for learning, as there is for the forward somersault. Second, there is a great tendency to lean excessively backwards when attempting the backward somersault, and a certain amount of fear increases this tendency. Obviously this can lead to a painful separation between performer and trampoline. Third, the half-way-over landing that might be the result of panic, change of mind, or not enough rotational throw is much less compatible with the laugh-it-off-and-try-again procedure than is the comparable landing in the forward somersault. All this is not designed to discourage you from learning "the back," but only to make you aware of the importance of getting some capable help and to prevent you from being foolhardy because you are unaware of the dangers.

An expert teacher can teach backward somersaults without a safety belt by grasping (at the waist) the clothing of the one he is teaching, bouncing with him on preliminary bounces, then staying on the bed as the somersaulter goes into his attempted "back," lifting, turning, and supporting him as he needs it. The teacher has to know when the bouncer is going to "go for it" and know how to avoid killing his bounce and how to handle most effectively his weight and assist his rotation. It is not a job for the inexperienced. To learn to hand spot in this manner, the teacher should practice on someone who is already confident and sure of the stunt and thereby gain experience before trying to spot someone who really needs it.

To teach with safety belts is much more satisfactory and requires less skill. The hand-belt is a strong leather or canvas belt with a strong fastener and with ropes suspended from each side. When these ropes are held by strong assistants on each side of the trampoline (standing level with the bed), the bouncer can try low somersaults with safety. The overhead-suspended belt is much the most satisfactory and is recommended for use whenever it can possibly be made available. Such an arrangement is accomplished by running the ropes from the sides of the belt through high overhead pulley blocks and down so that one assistant has both ropes in his hands to control the weight of the somersaulter. With this kind of belt, also, it is best for the spotter to learn to take care of novices by practicing on experienced subjects who can already do the stunt, until he learns to keep the slack out of the lines and to stop the performer in mid-air at will. Belts, ropes, pulleys, supports, and information about them are available from any of the major trampoline manufacturers.

Stunt No. 38—TUCKED BACKWARD SOMERSAULT

DESCRIPTION OF ACTION. As the spring of the trampoline lifts you into the air you thrust your hips forward in the same way, but more forcefully, as you do for the first motion of the sit drop (Stunt No. 4). At the same time your arms are swinging forward and upward to an overhead reach (Fig. 38a). It is not necessary or advisable to lean backward but only to tip backward. Thus, as your shoulders pull backward your hips move an equal amount forward so that the center of your weight stays over the point of take-off and you will not travel backwards.

After achieving this stretch position and riding it briefly, you start to bend your knees and bend at the waist and drop your hands to the hands-on-shins tuck position, similar to the corresponding position in the tucked forward somersault. Your head should go way back either as you tuck or before. You look back as far as you can, trying to see the trampoline bed and the spot on which you intend to land (Fig. 38b).

The opening from the tuck to a stand-up landing is done fairly quickly when you determine by sight that you are about three-quarters of the way around on your somersault. Thus the last quarter of rotation will be slower and will permit you to make

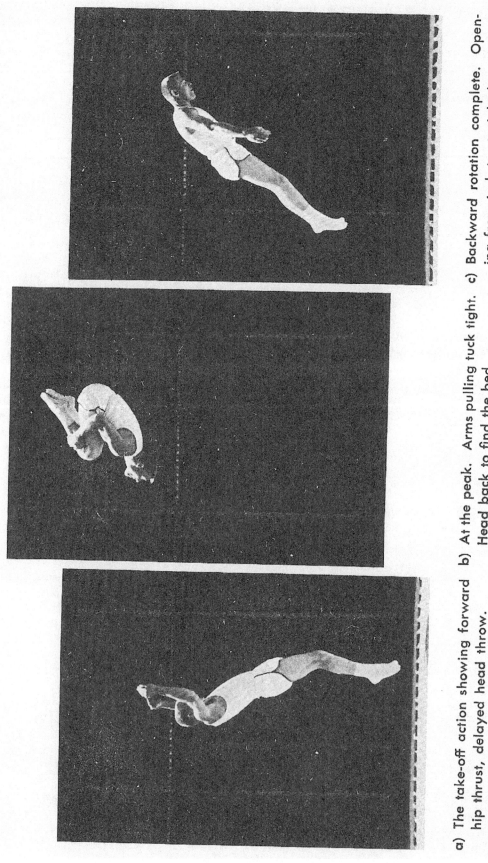

a) The take-off action showing forward   b) At the peak.   Arms pulling tuck tight.   c) Backward rotation complete.   Open-
   hip thrust, delayed head throw.   Head back to find the bed.   ing from tuck to straight has slowed
                                                                                     rotation.   Ready to land on the feet.

Fig. 38.   Tucked backward somersault.

what adjustments are necessary to land in balance to stop or to bounce again (Fig. 38c).

STEPS IN LEARNING

1. Before trying to learn the tucked backward somersault, you should have had a lot of trampoline experience. In addition to many other stunts, you will especially need to know the tucked bounce, the sit drop (with forward hip thrust), the back drop, the hands-and-knees drop, the back pullover, and the tucked forward somersault.

2. Learn a modification of the back drop (layout style) which starts with a strong forward hip thrust into an arch, then changes to a bent-body back landing. Learn to do this without traveling backwards.

3. Practice lying flat on your back, then suddenly bend into a tuck, pulling up on your shins and back with your head.

4. Now with some dependable support for your safety, such as a safety belt or an experienced hand spotter (see the introductory paragraphs of this chapter), try the backward somersault from a modest bounce. The first move is like the beginning of the layout-style back drop of Step 2, above. This is followed quickly by the change into the tuck and looking back to find the bed. Be content to get over to your hands and knees at first. Don't try too hard. Take it easy.

5. When you are consistently getting over to your feet with a minimum of assistance (10 out of 10 tries) and are confident you can do it alone, you can discard your safety devices and take a try. If you run into difficulties in the form of excessive fear, failure to complete the somersault, or dangerous traveling, get back into the safety belt to iron out your troubles.

CORRECTION OF ERRORS

A. One of the most common and treacherous mistakes is the failure to push the hips forward and pull the shoulders back right after the take-off. This backward bending movement is your insurance against stalling in mid-air and consequently crashing onto your head. More practice on the layout back drop can help to cure this defect.

B. Traveling backwards instead of going straight up is the result of getting the center of your weight behind your take-off point as you are being lifted by the trampoline. If the amount of travel is more than a few feet, it can be dangerous. The cause is often the placing of the feet at a point considerably ahead of the place where they have been bouncing when making the last landing before the somersault. Traveling can be caused by failing to move the hips forward when bending backwards at the start of the somersault. To correct, practice spotting or gaining sit drops and layout back drops (i.e., those which land even with, or ahead of, the take-off point).

C. The third critical error committed frequently on this stunt is the failure to use the head and eyes in such a manner as to aid rotation and insure control. This may be in the form of failing to put the head way back or in the form of keeping the eyes closed while turning over. In either case, concentration on these details while practicing in the belt should serve to correct the error.

Stunt No. 39—TRAMPOLINE BACKWARD SOMERSAULT

DESCRIPTION IN ACTION. This particular style of backward somersault is commonly called a "tramp back" and could be briefly described as a semi-tucked backward somersault designed to be most efficient in "swing" routines; i.e., in bouncing directly from one stunt to another. It is neither open nor tucked, but somewhere in between. As you leave the bed, the arms swing upward and somewhat outward, the body tips backward, and the knees start bending forward and upward (Fig. 39a). Your head does not throw back during this action, but remains in a forward-looking position until the peak of the lift. As the top is reached, the head is snapped back, the body may be doubled up more and swings between the upward reaching arms (Fig. 39b). As you sight the bed, your body and legs begin to unbend while you rotate to a facing-downward position (Fig. 39c). The arms have remained near their original upward position while the body has swung through between them so that now they are trailing well behind the body ready for a strong beat as you come in for a rebound into another somersault or variation thereof. The first contact with the bed on the landing is made while the body is apparently leaning forward. The body comes to a vertical position, however, during the lowering and raising of the bed so that the next take-off can be straight up and the series of stunts will stay over the center of the trampoline.

STEPS IN LEARNING

I. Learn the orthodox tucked backward somersault (Stunt No. 38) before undertaking to learn this special variation.

2. To get the "feel" of this motion, the hanging rings in the gymnasium or on the playground will be most helpful. The action is like a skin-the-cat on the rings. If you can jump and pull yourself through the positions described above while hanging on the rings, you will have done a very close imitation of the trampoline stunt which you are learning.

3. The safety belt will be a big time-saver in the mastery of this stunt and, of course, is a must if you are attempting to learn this stunt before its predecessor, the tucked backward somersault.

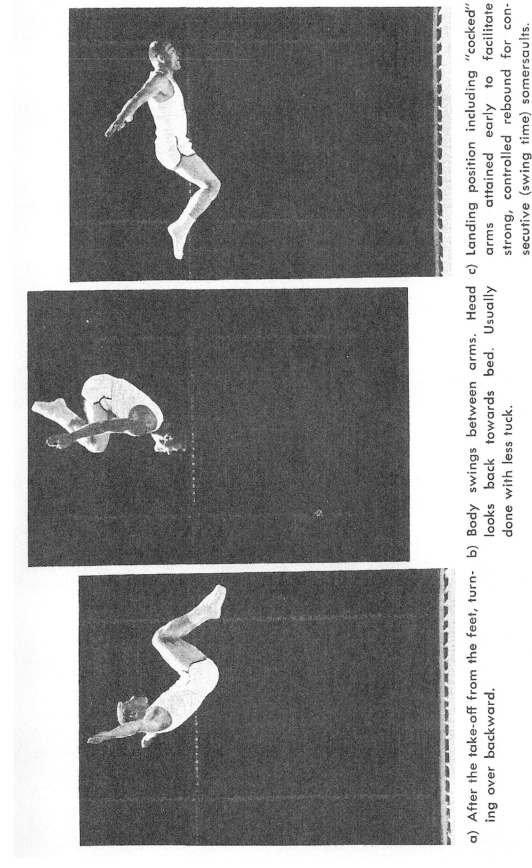

a) After the take-off from the feet, turn- b) Body swings between arms. Head c) Landing position including "cocked"
ing over backward.   looks back towards bed. Usually   arms attained early to facilitate
                                            done with less tuck.   strong, controlled rebound for con-
                                                                                   secutive (swing time) somersaults.

Fig. 39. Trampolin backward somersault.

4. In learning to swing out of this stunt, use easier and safer stunts at first until you are sure of yourself, then see if you can swing into a forward somersault from this backward somersault and, many successes later, you can try for two backward somersaults in swing time.

CORRECTION OF ERRORS

A. Being overanxious to bring the knees up into the semi-tuck may result in killing or losing part of your spring. Be sure you get the full leg drive accomplished before letting the knees bend.

B. Putting the head back early instead of delaying it is not a serious error. Some good trampolinists do it that way. The head-delay style has the advantage of better sight control and less tendency to dizziness.

C. A sluggish turn-over can often be corrected by a more vigorous backward shoulder pull and backward overhead arm thrust. It is important to get turned over early to have more time to adjust for the combined landing-and-take-off.

Stunt No. 40—OPEN BACKWARD SOMERSAULT

DESCRIPTION OF ACTION. At the very beginning of the lift you start the backward-bending action which gives your body its rotation. The arms, of course, have swung through their usual down beat as you were landing and sinking into the bed and are swinging forward and upward as you are on your way up into your somersault. As you bend backward at the waist, you pull your bent arms back above your shoulders at about head level and start laying your head back as far as you can, looking for the landing area (Fig. 40a). The knees are allowed to bend during this turn-over to speed up the rotation, but the body position remains arched during almost the whole stunt. Since the shoulders travel backward early and at a fast rate, the hips must move forward of the starting position equally quickly in order to prevent the flight of the somersault from moving markedly backward.

The open-body rotation, with the arms bent and close to the body and the head pulling back strongly, continues (Fig. 40b) until you are about three-quarters of the way around and are therefore in the air, front side down, several feet above the bed and parallel to it. At this point you stop pulling back in the arched position, fix your eyes on the bed ahead of your landing spot, bend at the waist, lengthen out your arms and prepare for a landing or rebound as the case may be (Fig. 40c).

This style of backward somersault is an important and useful step in your progress toward more advanced somersaults and especially twisting backward somersaults. It is not meant to be especially high, but is meant to turn over quickly and to be spotted; i.e., have its landing very near the same spot as its take-off.

a) Soon after take-off from feet, showing whip-like backward throw.

b) After half of somersault. Body position is the same. Arms are dropping.

c) The break at the waist preceding the landing.

Fig. 40. Open backward somersault.

STEPS IN LEARNING

1. Extensive, successful trampoline experience is essential before stunts like this should be attempted.

2. If you have learned well the tucked back somersault or tramp back, or both, you may be able gradually to modify the style of one of them to develop this open form. Combined with determination and patience, the help of someone to tell you when you are getting something like the right position will bring success. Assuming the correct body-arched, head-back, arms-bent position while kneeling on the trampoline or floor is a good way to familiarize yourself with the desired position.

3. With an overhead-suspension safety belt and an experienced operator on the other end, the open somersault can be learned either with or without previous backward somersault experience. The first step with the belt is to take a small bounce, lay back strongly with head and arms and body-arch on the take-off, and come down in a front-landing position. after turning over three-quarters of a turn backwards. The arch is held all the way. The belt-rope handler must carry most of the burden and let the performer down easily on his front, or hold him up if he is not coming down correctly.

4. After Step 3 has been practiced repeatedly and successfully, the next step is to try the same movement, a little higher but just as forcefully, and then, when over the bed in the horizontal open-landing position, to change quickly to a hands-and-feet pyramid landing or a hands-and-knees landing. Be sure the open position is held as long as possible before changing for the landing.

5. Now with a little more height, or a little more force, the last-minute change can be made by bending at the waist to a stand-up landing instead of a hands-and-feet or hands-and-knees one. Thus the open backward somersault in the belt will have been accomplished.

6. When you are consistently doing good open somersaults without traveling backward or forward more than a foot or two, and are confident that you can do the same thing without the safety belt, you are ready to undo the buckle and go it alone. If your solo is unsuccessful, get back into the belt and, if necessary, start over with Step 3.

CORRECTION OF ERRORS

A. Failure to keep the weight centered over the take-off point, and the consequent traveling, is a most common fault in this stunt also. Practice sliding the hips forward on a take-off into a gaining sit drop or layout back drop, and then try to carry the same action into your somersault attempt. Avoid setting the feet down ahead of their bouncing spot when you are placing them for the somersault take-off.

E. A slow-moving rotation can be corrected by a stronger and earlier backward head-throw, arm-pull, and body-bend. Drive with the legs. Do not let them buckle while throwing this backward whip.

C. If the open part of the somersault does not endure for about three-quarters of the turnover, you are not yet doing the stunt correctly. Try to hold it all the way to overcorrect the error of bending too soon.

Stunt No. 41-TUCKED BACKWARD ONE-AND-ONE-QUARTER SOMERSAULT

DESCRIPTION OF ACTION. The take-off from the feet, the forward hip thrust and overhead reach, and the change to the hands-on-shins tuck position are the same as described for the Tucked Backward Somersault (Fig. 41a). Instead of opening out of your tuck after three-quarters of a somersault as you do when you wish to land on your feet, you now hold your tuck (Fig. 41b), rotating on past the full somersault. Then release your legs, straighten them, reach down and back behind your hips and come to a sit landing (Fig. 41c). From this landing, you bounce up to a stand.

STEPS IN LEARNING

1. The tucked backward somersault is, of course, a prerequisite to this stunt, as is the sit drop.

2. If you can do the prerequisite stunts with ease, you will not need the belt to learn this stunt. Don't try for extra rotation; just hold your tuck longer.

3. You can, by rotating a little harder and holding your tuck a little longer, come to a back landing instead of the sit. Learn the one quarter to sit landing first and then, as your courage permits, go ahead and learn the one-and-a-third to a kick-out back drop landing and rebound. The extra rotation can be gained by a more vigorous forward hip thrust and backward shoulder pull at the beginning of the stunt.

CORRECTION OF ERRORS

A. Failure to correctly execute the initial stretch and the tuck because of over concern about the new landing position is not an uncommon fault. It is the result of trying this new stunt without a sufficient mastery of the single tucked somersault. If the correct somersault movements have become well-established habits before you attempt the back one quarter, they will not disappear in panic when the new element is introduced.

B. Opening from the tuck too soon will result in hitting the feet before the seat. This makes a recovery to a stand on the next bounce very difficult. Hold the tuck until the opening legs will

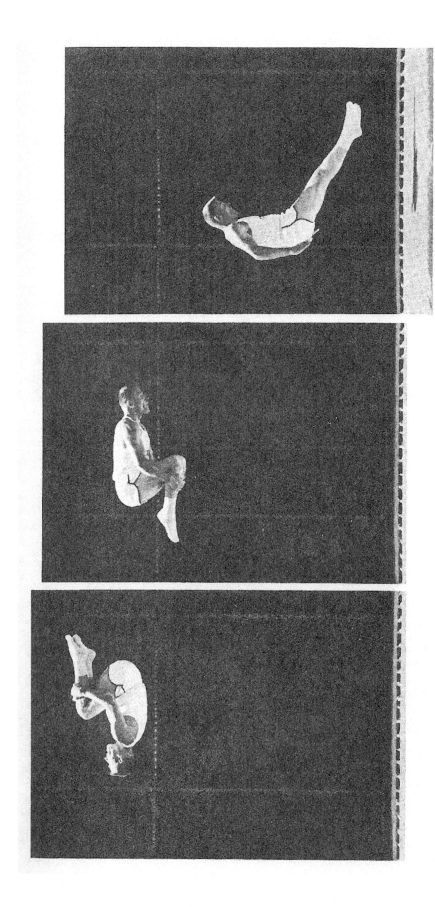

a) Part way over with a tight tuck.　　b) Still holding the tuck to prolong back-　c) The somersault completed. Ready
　　　　　　　　　　　　　　　　　　　ward rotation.　　　　　　　　　　　　for the sit landing.

Fig. 41.　Tucked backward one-and-one-quarter somersault.

land flat and the hands can be placed behind the hips with fingers pointing toward the feet and with the arms slightly bent.

Stunt No. 42—LAYOUT BACKWARD SOMERSAULT (Swan Style)

DESCRIPTION OF ACTION. This style of backward somersault does not differ very greatly from the open backward somersault (Stunt No. 40). There are some important differences, however, which set it off as a separate stunt. The strong, body-arched, head-back throw, with and after the take-off, is similar to the open back, but the preliminary bounces are usually higher, the arms are thrown out into a swan position and the knees are kept as straight as possible (Fig. 42a). The straight-knee, head-back, arched-body swan position is held all the way around (see Fig. 42b). Before the landing, the head-pull eases up and the arms drop down a bit for balance, but the body and knees stay as straight as possible until the last moment (Fig. 42c) when the knees bend a little to take up the landing shock. This is a form stunt, an imitation of the backward somersault straight as done by competitive springboard divers, and is not a good stunt to swing out of into other somersaults.

STEPS IN LEARNING

1. The open backward somersault (Stunt No. 40) and the swan bounce (Fig. 3a) should be learned before the layout or swan form of the backward somersault is attempted.

2. Another and easier variety of layout somersault can be used as a stepping-stone between the open back and the swan-style layout back. In this intermediate style, the body, legs, and head are used in the same manner as described above for the layout, but the arms are carried stretched tight down along the body and front of the thighs during the turnover.

3. When you are able to keep the knees nearly straight and hold the straight body position until the landing on the arms-down type of somersault described in Step 2, then you will, with a little more height, force, and practice be able to do it with your arms out in the swan position.

CORRECTION OF ERRORS

A. To attempt to do this stunt by riding to the height of the lift and then arching back is to guarantee failure. The backward rotation must be begun with a very forceful backward bending pull before your feet leave the bed.

B. Breaking at the waist in the late phases of the somersault may be a result of insufficient throw or of stopping the head and shoulder pull too soon. Do not stop your head and shoulders when your eyes sight the bed, but continue to pull all the way, as though you were going to start around again.

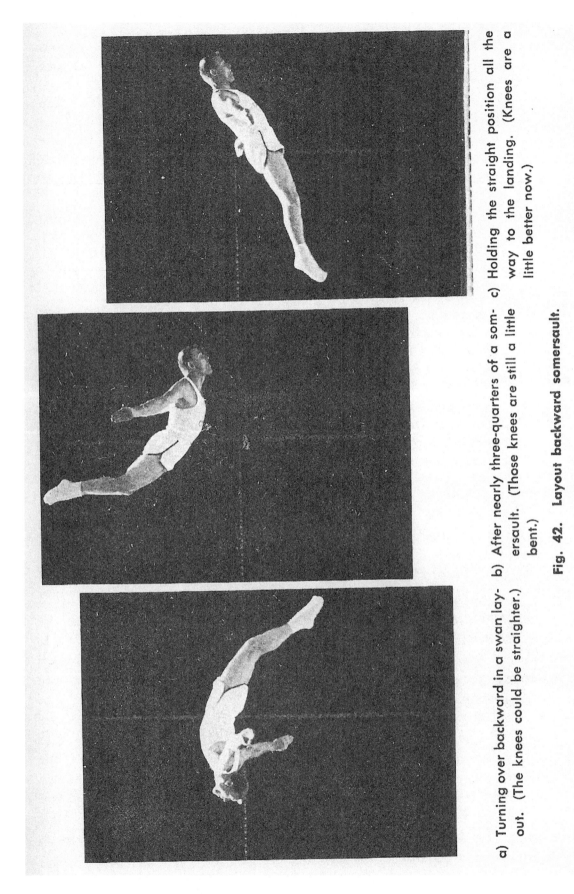

a) Turning over backward in a swan layout. (The knees could be straighter.)

b) After nearly three-quarters of a somersault. (Those knees are still a little bent.)

c) Holding the straight position all the way to the landing. (Knees are a little better now.)

Fig. 42. Layout backward somersault.

C. Bending the knees slightly during the turnover is a fault that shows up more in still pictures than in action, the complete elimination of which is desirable, but very difficult. (The author obviously hasn't mastered it yet; see Figs. 42a and 42b).

Stunt No. 43—OPEN HALF-BACK SOMERSAULT
(Open Backward Turnover to Front Landing)

DESCRIPTION OF ACTION. The take-off is much the same as for the open backward somersault (Stunt No. 40) in that the body is bent backward and the head looks back as far as possible. The arms do not reach overhead, but stop on their upward swing at about head level and let the rotating body more or less catch up to them (Fig. 43a). The strength of the backward throw is less than that for an open somersault of the same height so that the rotation will be slower. When the body has turned to the inverted vertical position (Fig. 43b), the eyes are fixed on the bed, the arms are dropping closer to the body and the amount of arch is increased or lessened to insure a level landing. As you come near the mat, you reach your arms forward, let your knees bend and flatten out for a front landing (Fig. 43c). From the front landing you bounce to your feet as in the front drop.

STEPS IN LEARNING

1. In the area of fundamentals, a thorough acquaintance with all varieties of front-landing stunts is an important preliminary to learning the halfback. The open back somersault (Stunt No. 40) should also be considered a prerequisite to this more treacherous stunt.

2. Even if you are an experienced back somersaulter, it is most advisable to use the safety belt to learn the half-back. In the belt, try it from a low bounce with a quick layback first and then, still in the belt, gradually do them higher and proportionately slower until you are able to do them comfortably, confidently, and consistently hom a medium-high bounce.

3. When you first try the half-back without the belt, remember that it is better to overturn it a little bit than to under turn it. Be prepared to change quickly to a hands-and-knees landing if you find that you are overturned.

CORRECTION OF ERRORS

A. Avoiding overturn and underturn is, of course, a matter of using approximately the right amount of force in the initial backward bending movement. Some adjusting corrections can be made in mid-air, however, if you learn to see as soon as you can how far over you are and either arch harder to increase your rotation or bend forward a little to check your rotation.

B. Traveling backward along the bed is an even more serious fault in this stunt than in the complete somersaults since landing off

a) The head leads the backward straight-body turnover.

b) Still turning backward, the eyes have located the bed. Adjustments for landing can now be made.

c) The body is still rotating so that it will be level by the time it sinks into the bed. Rebound from front landing to feet will complete the stunt.

Fig. 43. Open half-back somersault.

the bed in a front-landing position can be most uncomfortable. Use the forward hip movement with the backward shoulder pull to keep the center of mass over the point of take-off. Until you are able to do this on the open backward somersault, you should certainly not be trying the half-back.

C. Improper position on the front landing can result in an uncomfortable or even an injurious landing. Be sure the forearms are in the semi-reach position and are helping to catch and support the weight and that the excessive arch is removed from the back before landing.

Stunt No. 44-TUCKED CODY
(Tucked Backward Somersault from Front Landing)

DESCRIPTION OF ACTION. The front landing from which the cody begins is usually reached either by tipping forward as in the front drop (Fig. 44a) or by turning over backward to it as in the half-back (Stunt No. 43). In either case it is important that just before the front landing there is a slight bending at your waist, that your knees hit a little before the chest and arms (Fig. 44b), and that the knees start to bend as the contact is made and continue to bend during the on-the-bed interval.

As you are leaving the bed from your front landing, you push down forcefully and continually with your arms and hands as long as you have contact (Fig. 44c). At the same time you pull the head back as far and as hard as you can and start bending at the waist toward the tuck. Before you are very far off the bed, you should have grasped your shins and begun to pull in with your arms (Fig. 44d). You continue to pull your tuck tighter and lay your head back (Fig. 44e) until you have turned completely over backward and are ready to open out and land on your feet (Fig. 44f).

STEPS IN LEARNING

1. Excellent control of high front drops (and the half-back if you wish to use it as a preliminary to the cody) is one of the essential skills prerequisite to the learning of the cody. Doing the front drop to back drop with facility and being sure and skillful with tucked back somersaults are also necessary before you are ready for this stunt.

2. Prepare yourself for trying the cody by practicing high front drops with the special cody landing described above, by practicing low front drops to back drops with special emphasis on strong push away and early tuck, and by practicing low tucked back somersaults with an effort to fully utilize the head pull and tight tuck to get over.

3. Your first full attempts at doing the cody should be done either in the safety belt or with an experienced hand spotter. The belt handler has to cope with the problem of more take-up on the rope between the take-off and the landing, since the

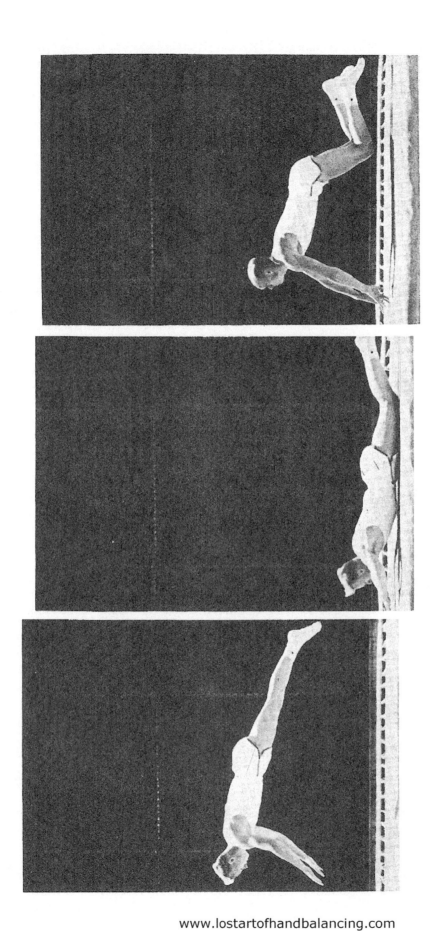

a) Just before the front landing. Note b) First contact on the front landing. c) After sinking into the bed and being
   slight bend at waist, arms reaching   Note legs hitting bed before chest   lifted up. Note the hand push-away
   for bed, feet lower than head.   and arms. Knees starting to bend.   and the early doubling-up.

Fig. 44.   Tucked cody (demonstrated by Ron Graham).

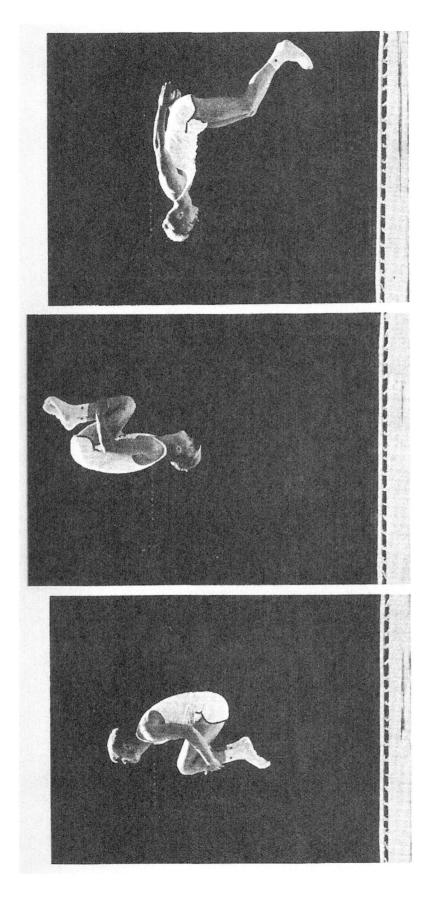

d) Soon after leaving the bed, turning over backward, grasping tuck.

e) Still turning, still tucked.

f) Somersault nearly completed. Opening and preparing for landing on the feet. Note arms swinging back for the beat for the next take-off.

Fig. 44. Continued.

performer goes so Iowan the take-off position. The hand spotter should stand on the side of the trampoline and rush in to catch, spin or otherwise assist the performer after the front landing. The key to effective hand spotting is to move in close and use both arms under the performer if much support is needed.

4. As is true for most stunts, you will be ready to solo when you have proved your ability to complete the stunt successfully and safely many successive times and you yourself feel that you can do the same thing without the protection of the spotter.

CORRECTION OF ERRORS

A. The most common difficulty with this stunt is the inability to get sufficient backward rotation to get you over to the feet on the somersault. The causes of this defect are most likely some or all of the following: Failure to bend at the waist a little before landing on the front and to land knees before chest; failure to bend the knees while landing; failure to push early, strongly, and continuously downward with the arms and hands; failure to start the head pull and the tucking action immediately on leaving the bed; failure to keep pulling the knees close to the chest by pulling on the shins all the way over.

B. Taking this stunt too lightly and first trying it without protection is a mistake which could be serious. Landing on the back of the neck with the weight of the hips to add force to the jackknifing action is one of the most dangerous trampoline landings I can think of. Even moderate altitude and the give of the bed are not enough to keep this halfway-over landing from being a dangerous one. So, use the safety belt, have a really competent hand spotter, or skip the stunt entirely.

ADDITIONAL BACKWARD SOMERSAULT STUNTS LISTED:

1. Backward three-quarters somersault to hands-and-knees landing

2. Piked backward somersault

3. Backward somersault from a sit drop

4. Backward one-and-a-quarter somersault to back pullover

5. Backward one-and-a-third somersault to back drop

6. Tucked half-back somersault

7. Jackknife half-back somersault

8. Backward somersault from hands-and-knees landing

9. Backward somersault from back landing to back landing

10. Tucked backward one-and-a-half somersault from front drop to back drop (one-and-a-half cody)

8

Twisting Somersaults

When you add to the forward or backward turnover a twist around
the body's long axis, you have some variety of twisting
somersault. A vertical jump, turning around to face the opposite
direction while in the air (180-degree turn) without tipping
forward or backward is a half twist with no somersault. Twice
that much twist would be a full twist and would end you up facing
the same direction from which you started. Now, if you turn all
the way over in a somersault while you are doing this 360-degree
lateral twist, you have done a full twisting somersault. This
obviously opens up a wide field of possible stunts. There are
forward somersaults with twists and backward somersaults with
twists. There are half twists and triple twists and all the half-
twist multiples in between. There are some preceded by tucks,
some by pikes, and some done with straight body all the way. In
addition, of course, there are various fractions and multiples of
turnovers or somersaults and various landing and take-off
positions. When you figure all the possible combinations of these
elements the results are staggering. Doing them all would, of
course, be more so.

I have selected six of the most representative of the twisters to
picture and describe in detail. From these you can learn
principles of performing and teaching twisters which will aid you
in learning, or helping others to learn, many additional twisting
somersaults, some of which are listed at the end of this chapter,
some of which are mentioned in Chapter 9, and many of which you
can figure out for yourself.

With adequate preparation and gradual progression, twisting
somersaults can be learned without belts. The ordinary safety
belt can be used for twisters by wrapping the ropes around the
body a half or full turn before starting the stunt so that after
the twist is accomplished they will have a straight pull. This
procedure is not altogether successful as the wrapped-around
ropes oftentimes get in the way of the performer's arms and legs.
The "twisting belt" is the most satisfactory safety device for
learning these stunts. It consists of two metal rings around the

body separated by ball bearings. The inner ring is attached to the performer, the outer ring to the ropes, and they are held firmly together by the structure of the outer ring. This device enables you to twist around as many times as you wish or are able. The inner part of the belt twists with you while the outer part remains as it was without turning. Thus, no preliminary wrapping of the ropes is necessary to prevent them twisting around each other when you twist, and entanglement with the ropes is much less likely. Since Charley Pond, coach of gymnastics at the University of Illinois, devised this piece of equipment several years ago, the learning of advanced twisting somersaults has been greatly facilitated. As far as I know these twisting belts are made only by Fred Medart Products, Inc., of St. Louis, Missouri.

Stunt No. 45—HALF TWISTING TUCKED FORWARD SOMERSAULT

DESCRIPTION OF ACTION. The take-off and the first movements of this twisting somersault are just the same as for the tucked forward somersault (Stunt No. 29), except that there should be an attempt to bend forward a little sooner and more forcefully and tuck earlier to speed up the spin (Fig. 45a). When you have held the tuck position a little more than halfway over, you open out forcefully in a forward and upward direction straightening the knees and opening at the waist with a hip-twisting action (Fig. 45b). During this straightening, hip-twisting action the head is not at once turned, but continues to face toward the feet. As your body straightens, the upper body follows the hips in their twisting action. When you are stretched out and have rolled over about 90 degrees, you turn your head around to look at the bed, continue to roll, and then bend at the waist to prepare for a landing (Fig. 45c). The action of the arms is not a great factor in this particular twist, but they should stay fairly close to the body axis in order not to impede the twist. The landing is made in a standing position facing the opposite direction from that which you were facing when you began the somersault.

STEPS IN LEARNING

1. Prerequisite stunts include the tucked forward somersault and the half twist from back drop (Stunt No. 18), specifically, with a strong recommendation for much additional forward somersault work and other twisting stunts such as the early twisting cradle (Stunt No. 22) and the cat twist (Stunt No. 36).

2. Practice many forward somersaults, trying particularly to bend and tuck early, spin fast, and kick out early in order to have a long drop in the straight position.

3. Practice the half twist from back drop many times, thinking of the possibility of using the same twisting kick-out action in mid-air from the somersault start. Also, from lying on your back on the trampoline bed in a hands-on-shins tuck position, practice some twisting kick-outs to a sort of on-the-side landing.

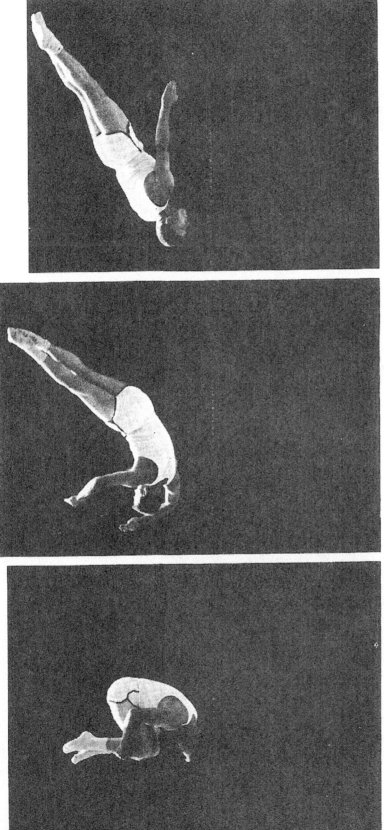

a) Rotating forward after take-off from the feet. Still on the way up. Somersault nearly three-quarters finished.

b) The hip-twisting upward kick-out from the tuck. Note head is not yet twisted.

c) The half twist is complete. Now the body will bend a little and rotation will bring the body around to a stand-up finish.

Fig. 45. Half twisting tucked forward somersault.

4. Now if you have the use of a twisting belt, just get in it and do the stunt. Be sure there is a responsible party on the other end of the rope. If you are learning without belt, you should at first try only a quarter hip-twist, late in the somersault, just before landing.

5. The final success is gained either by taking off the belt if you have used one and doing the stunt by yourself or by edging your way into the stunt gradually without the use of the belt. You progress from the very late quarter hip-twist described in Step 4 to an earlier and more complete twist until you achieve the 180-degree twist as pictured and described.

CORRECTION OF ERRORS

A. Trying to get in some of the twist when starting the somersault is an error that can get you all mixed up and spoils the stunt. Don't twist at all until you are kicking out of your tuck.

B. Twisting the head and shoulders first when coming out of the tuck is another common source of difficulty. Don't try to look around immediately to see where you are going to land. Watch your legs extend with their twisting motion, then look around. This will insure the domination of the hip twist over the shoulder twist, which is proper for this stunt.

C. Insufficient somersault spin or insufficient height can cause you to fall short of a good landing. Increase spin by earlier and more forceful bending and tucking. But do not tuck before you complete your takeoff leg drive.

D. Holding your tuck too far around can make it difficult or impossible to complete the half twist before landing. Spin fast and kick out early.

Stunt No. 46-BARANI

DESCRIPTION OF ACTION. From a regular arm-circling bounce, you take off with the arm beat and, at the same time, you bend forward at the waist much as in the piked forward somersault except that you do not duck your head and you spread your arms out laterally (Fig. 46a). There should be a little shoulder twist to the left (or right) in this forward bend, but the principal effort of this first movement is the forward bending to get the somersault rotation started. Without taking the eyes off the bed, you swing your right arm across past your knee (assuming a left twist). Your shoulders turn with the arm swing (Fig. 46b). Now you open out at the waist from the pike to a straight position, and as you do so your hips follow the twist initiated by the shoulders. Your arms drop down close along your body in order not to hamper either somersault rotation or twist (Fig. 46c). You continue to watch the same spot on the bed all the way. When the half twist is complete and you are somewhere near horizontal over

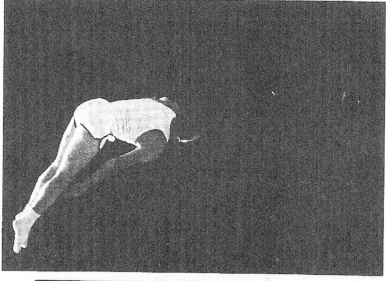

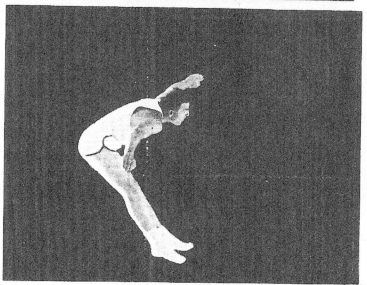

a) After taking off from the feet with forward bend. Note arms are wide and head is up.

b) At this point the shoulders have twisted more than the hips. The un-bending at the waist has started; the right arm is swinging past the knees to aid the left twist.

c) The body has been straight and is bending again. The twist is almost complete.

Fig. 46. Barani.

the bed, you bend at the waist and come down on your feet. Thus you have in reality done a half twisting piked forward somersault, but without ever ducking the head or looking away from the bed. Considered another way, the barani is like the tumbling stunt called a roundoff, but done from a two-foot take-off and without putting the hands down. The barani is a most useful trampoline stunt.

STEPS IN LEARNING

1. You should have an extensive background of fundamental stunts in your bag of tricks before you try to add the barani to your list of accomplishments. Forward somersaults, especially the piked forward somersault, will also be most helpful. It is not necessary to have learned any backward somersaults before learning the barani, but the half twisting forward somersault would be a great asset.

2. If you are able to do the stunts listed in Step 1, you can learn the barani readily without the use of the safety belt. One very successful progression involves the review of the half twisting tucked forward somersault and then the learning of the half twisting piked forward somersault which is just the same except that the forward somersault part is done with straight knees and bent body as in the piked forward somersault (Stunt No. 30) and the twisting kick-out is replaced by a hip-twisting opening from the pike position. The final step in this series is gradually to learn to do the half twisting piked forward somersault without grasping under the legs on the pike and without ducking the head at any time. This, then, is a barani.

3. Another progression which can be used even without a background of forward somersaults, plain or twisting, starts by doing a drop to a knee landing, bouncing to a quarter-turned momentary handstand support on the bed, then continuing to turn another quarter twist as you snap down from the handstand to a knee landing facing back toward the end of the bed from which you came. The second phase of this progression requires the same action, but without touching the hands to the mat on the way over from knees to knees. Finally when this knees toknees barani is learned or nearly learned, the same action can be attempted from feet to feet. The progression outlined in Step 2 is a better one for those who are ready for it.

4. If the safety belt is used in learning the barani, it must be either a twisting belt or an ordinary belt with the ropes wrapped around the waist so that they will be straight during the last part of the stunt. When you are learning in the belt, either of the progressions indicated above may be used, or you can simply try to do the completed stunt as pictured and described without the preliminary stunts.

CORRECTION OF ERRORS

A. Getting a lot of twist with the shoulders at the beginning of the stunt is an error that must be avoided to achieve success. You should make your first forward-bending action with only a very little twist. To correct the early twisting tendency you should go to the other extreme trying not to twist at all until you are opening from the bend.

B. Another common tendency is an attempt to kick your feet up behind you as you leave the bed. This is a misdirected effort to get the feet through their arc and down to their landing. It results, instead, in a failure to get enough rotation and a consequent stalling in mid-air. Put the first emphasis on driving the hips up behind, in the same way as you do in the piked somersault, and you will get the forward turnover force you need.

Stunt No. 47—HALF TWISTING OPEN BACKWARD SOMERSAULT

DESCRIPTION OF ACTION. You start off with the same action as that for the open backward somersault (Stunt No. 40), except that you should be more forceful and your shoulders may be slightly turned in the direction of the intended half twist (Fig. 47a). Since a left turn is used in the illustration, we will describe it that way. The twist in this first part of the somersault is very slight. The main emphasis is on the somersaulting forces, and so the head is thrown straight back. When you are a little past half-way over, you forcefully twist your lower body, hips, and legs to the left without bending at the waist (Fig. 47b). The shoulders and head follow the hips around in the twist until you are facing opposite to your original direction, still in the open position, and ready to make your landing on your feet (Fig. 47c).

STEPS IN LEARNING

1. Before you start on this stunt you should be very proficient on the open backward somersault, should be able to do the layout backward somersault (Stunt No. 42), and should have reviewed the half twist to front drop (Stunt No. 17) which involves a similar hip twist.

2. Do a few open back somersaults with as strong a throw as that used for the layout back somersault so that you can keep a straight body until the landing.

3. Stand on the right foot (to practice for a left twist) on the floor with the body bent forward a little and the left leg pulled back to be in line with the trunk. Now twist the hips to the left pushing your mid-section forward as it twists, follow with your shoulders and head, and let the right foot twist on the floor. Step down with the left foot alongside of the right so you are standing facing the opposite direction from the starting position. This simulates, as well as you can without being in midair, the twisting action of the half twisting open back

a) Almost half of the backward turnover is finished with just a hint of a shoulder twist started.

b) Now the hips have twisted farther than the shoulders and are leading the twist. The head follows.

c) The shoulders and head have caught up with the hips and the half twist is complete. The body will rotate forward to the landing on the feet.

Fig. 47. Half twisting open backward somersault.

somersault.

4. Now try your strong-throw open back somersault and, just before landing, twist just your hips a quarter-turn to the left and land this way.

5. By gradually learning to twist a little earlier and a little earlier and gradually acquiring a slight twist on the beginning lay-back also, you will be able to work your way around to the complete half twist. The learning process may be shortened by using the safety belt, but it is not necessary if you have the prerequisite skills well in hand.

CORRECTION OF ERRORS

A. Trying to lead the twist with the head and shoulders will hamper your attempts to learn this stunt. Be sure you are throwing straight back with the head and almost straight back with the shoulders. When learning to get the hip-twist earlier and earlier, do not let it get earlier than the half-way-over point.

B. An insufficiently strong throw will make it necessary to bend at the waist in order to come in for a landing at about the time when you are trying to twist. The bent body and the twist do not go well together, so the twist will be incomplete. Throw the somersault strongly enough so that you can stay open all the way. An alternative style has a pike movement in it after the twist is more or less completed. This style involves a just-as-strong or stronger throw and a slightly earlier twist. The pike position comes in as a sit-up action between positions corresponding to Figs. 47b and 47c.

Stunt No. 48—FULL TWISTING FORWARD SOMERSAULT

DESCRIPTION OF ACTION. The first action of this stunt is a forward bend at the waist (Fig. 48a) with slightly twisting shoulders and trunk, much as in the barani (Stunt No. 46). During these first movements the arms are carried in a mildly sideward-reaching position. As the forward turnover progresses, the shoulders and trunk twist more (Fig. 48b), and the body begins to straighten. As it straightens, the hips and legs follow the shoulder twist (Fig. 48c) so that by the time the somersault is about five-eighths complete, the body has finished the half-twist much as in the barani (Fig. 48d). Now, to complete the other half-twist, you keep your body straight, pull in your arms close to your body axis and keep your eyes on the bed as your body continues to twist (Fig. 48e). Near the landing time you swing your head around to see the trampoline ahead of your landing spot (Fig. 48f). You land on your feet facing the same direction as you were facing when you began your somersault.

The foregoing description and the illustrations are of the head-up barani-type forward full twister. The alternative style is

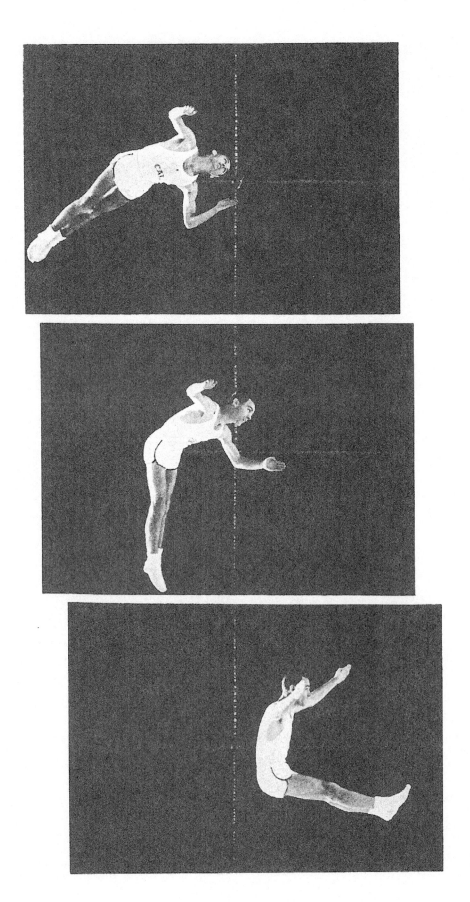

a) After the take-off from the feet, bend- b) The shoulder twist is toward the c) The body is straightening. The left
ing forward. right. The left shoulder is coming for- shoulder still coming forward. One-
ward. quarter twist accomplished.

Fig. 48. Full twisting forward somersault (demonstrated by Roger Adams).

d) A little past the half twist. Eyes have not lost the bed at any time. The hip twist is ahead of the shoulder twist.

e) Three-quarters of the somersault. Three-quarters of the twist. Still watching bed, hips still leading.

f) The hip twist is almost complete. Head is coming around. All will be straight by the landing.

Fig. 48. Continued.

done with the head ducked under as in the piked forward somersault, and then an opening twisting action as in the half twisting forward somersault, amplified by an arm throw from wide to close-in to complete the full twist. This second style is recommended for springboard divers to prepare them for the full twisting one-and-one-half forward somersault dive. The barani-type style is better for trampolinists since it permits the performer to watch the bed more of the time and therefore makes for better control. It is also a better preparation for the rudolph (Stunt No. 50).

STEPS IN LEARNING

1. It would be putting the cart before the horse to try to learn this stunt without first being able to do tucked and piked forward somersaults and a very good barani. Backward somersaults are not, however, essential as predecessors to the forward full twister. Of the non-somersault stunts, the barrel roll (Stunt No. 21), the corkscrew (Stunt No. 35), the cat twist (Stunt No. 36), and the double twist to back drop (Stunt No. 37) would all be useful to help you learn straight body twisting.

2. Review the barani (Stunt No. 46), using a particularly strong forward bending movement and a little more height than is usual so that you can do the entire last half of the stunt without bending at the waist.

3. Increase the amount of twist little by little in successive tries by turning your shoulders somewhat more vigorously directly after the straight-ahead bend-over and particularly by pulling the arms in close to the body axis after you have straightened out of your beginning pike. After some tries you should be able to work around to the full twist.

4. The twisting safety belt can be used to some advantage in learning this stunt. In some ways the belt is a hindrance and is by no means necessary for this stunt if you have the prerequisite stunts well learned.

CORRECTION OF ERRORS

A. Failure to get straight at the waist and knees and to keep straight while twisting are common causes of insufficient twist and are themselves many times the result of an insufficient somersault throw at the beginning. Make the initial body bend forceful and early so that enough rotation will be started to permit you to stay straight the rest of the way over to the landing.

B. Another cause of failure to complete the twist can be the incorrect use of the arms. Spreading them at the beginning and bringing them in close during the majority of the spin is of material assistance in obtaining maximum twist. In the close-in position, they may be down along the side, wrapped around the body or carried above the head. You may use a combination, putting one arm overhead and keeping the other alongside or around the body. Both the spread and the close-arm positions can be more exaggerated than is shown in the illustrations. Trampolinists such as Roger Adams (our demonstrator for this stunt) who can do triple twisters do not use their maximum twisting efficiency in doing a mere full twist.

Stunt No. 49—FULL TWISTING BACKWARD SOMERSAULT

DESCRIPTION OF ACTION. The take-off action is much the same as for a layout backward somersault (Stunt No. 42) with the strong backward shoulder pull and the forceful forward hip thrust and with the arms out in a swan-like position (Fig. 49a). The head, however, is not pulled back all the way but stops pulling when facing straight up. There is also a little twist started in the upper body with this essentially straight-back starting action. In this description, as in Roger Adams' photographic demonstration, the direction of the twist is to the right. By the time you have turned over one-quarter of a somersault, you will have turned your head and shoulders one-fourth turn to the right and your body will have followed (Fig. 49b). You continue to twist as you continue to rotate backward with straight body (Fig. 49c) so that by the time you have completed half a somersault you will have completed 180 degrees of twist. By this time, your arms are pulling in from their wide start to a close-to-the-body position. Also, by this time, your head has turned so that you can see the bed. You continue to see it during the remainder of the stunt.

During the interval between half and three-quarters of a somersault, you twist a little faster by keeping the arms in close and keeping the body straight (Figs. 49d and 49e). When the twist has been completed at about the three-quarter somersault stage (Fig. 49e), the body is bent at the waist and the arms are spread to stop the spin and come down to a balanced landing ready for a controlled stop or a rebound into another stunt (Fig. 49f). There are other acceptable styles of doing the "back full," but the one pictured and described here seems to combine smoothness, style, and control better than the others.

STEPS IN LEARNING

1. The layout backward somersault and the half twisting backward somersault are certainly necessary prerequisites to the full twisting back. In addition, the twisting non-somersault stunts recommended as preliminary to the full twisting forward somersaults (Stunt No. 48) will be useful in improving your twisting ability.

2. Using nearly the same technique as you do for the double twist to back drop (Stunt No. 37), learn to do a full twist to back drop. As compared to the double twist, you should use a lower bounce, more forward hip thrust, and a later look-around. Use the

a) From the feet take-off, the lay back is already twisting a little to the right (left shoulder forward). Head facing straight up.

b) Shoulders and head are leading the twist to the right.

c) Before half of the turnover has been done the twist is nearly half-complete. The eyes can see the bed.

Fig. 49. Full twisting backward somersault (demonstrated by Roger Adams).

d) Another half twist has taken place. e) With the twist almost complete, the f) Just before landing on the feet again. The head has finished its twist. body starts to bend.

Fig. 49. Continued.

arm action as described for the full twisting backward somersault.

3. The twisting safety belt is a big time-saver in learning the "back full." In the twisting belt, if you have the necessary stunts already learned as outlined in Steps I and 2 above, you can proceed directly now to the all-out attempt of the full twisting backward somersault. After many trials and corrections in line with the description and pictures, you may learn this stunt in a relatively short time (perhaps 30 or 40 trials in the belt).

4. Many trampolinists have learned the full twisting backward somersault without benefit of belt, and you can also if you have the prerequisites mastered. The procedure for learning without a belt is gradually to work your way around from the half-twisting back, fraction by fraction, until you can make it all the way. Then keep working on it to get the twist started earlier, and modify it to conform to the description and pictures presented here.

CORRECTION OF ERRORS

A. A common error is the tendency to throw for the twist without paying enough attention to somersault. This is particularly common to those who are learning in the safety belt. The cure is to over-correct by laying back straight (without twist) into the somersault and then start to twist by throwing the arm across and turning the head after you are part-way over.

B. Trying to twist while bent at the waist and the knees is an error which shows up in learning this stunt, as well as the other twisters we have described. The doubled-up twist is slower and more eccentric. A strong somersault action at the beginning will make it easier to keep straight.

C. Sometimes you may find that, after you have completed the twist, you cannot land on your feet but keep overturning and landing on your seat or back. Usually this is due to a combination of not seeing soon enough where you are and of bending at the waist too much and too soon after the twist is almost finished. Keeping the eyes on the trampoline bed during the twist and keeping the body straight until you see how much you need to bend it will generally cure this trouble.

D. Insufficient twist can be corrected by a more forceful or an earlier arm throw and head turn, and by keeping straight while twisting.

Stunt No. 50—RUDOLPH
(One-and-One-Half Twisting Forward Somersault)

DESCRIPTION OF ACTION. This stunt begins like a barani (Stunt No. 46) with a forward bend at the waist, without ducking the head, and with the arms extended forward and outward (Fig. 50a). There is a little shoulder and body twist to the left (or the right if you prefer to do the twist in that direction) in this first bend-over, but the emphasis is on the forward bend to get the turnover well started. On the way up, at approximately the time the body has tipped forward into a horizontal plane, the body is straightened and the right arm (for a left twist) is thrown down past the knees and both arms are brought in close to the chest (Fig. 50b). By the time the somersault is one-third complete, the head has turned with the twist and the body has completed 180 degrees or one-half of a full twist (Fig. 50c). You hold the same straight position with your head in such a position that you can see the bed (Fig. 50d) during another 360 degrees of twist until you are about three-fourths of the way through the somersault and are facing the bed with the front side of your body (a little later than Fig. 50e). At this point you bend at the waist and open your arms for a landing or drop them behind you for a rebound (Fig. 50f). Our demonstrator for this stunt, Ron Graham, is an excellent swing time bouncer and so his arms are preparing for the next take-off.

STEPS IN LEARNING

1. Many twisting stunts such as the barrel roll (Stunt No. 21), the corkscrew (Stunt No. 35), and the double twist to back drop (Stunt No. 37) should have been learned and reviewed before trying to learn the Rudolph. The half twisting forward somersault, the barani, and the full twisting forward somersault are necessary prerequisites to this one-and-one-half twisting forward somersault.

2. Use the full twisting forward somersault as your base of operations and, little by little on successive tries, add more twist to it until you can make it around to the one-and-one-half. To add this extra half twist to the full twister, you should do your initial pike with your arms wider, straighten sooner, throw your arm sooner and more forcefully, and wrap-up tighter (i.e., keep your arms in closer).

3. Use of the twisting belt for learning this stunt is a time-saver and an injury-preventer for many. The belt and ropes do hamper your action some, however, and consequently many who have the belt available learn this stunt without using it. If difficulties develop, however, it's most helpful to use the belt in overcoming them.

CORRECTION OF ERRORS

A. Overturning the somersault and thus landing on the seat or the back is a common error during the learning procedure. The tendency is to throw more somersault as you try to throw more twist. Actually the rudolph requires less somersault rotation than does the full twisting forward somersault. To correct the overturn tendency, open sooner from the first bend-over, keep

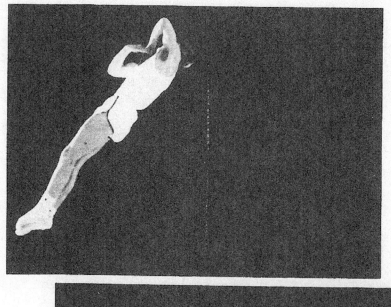

a) After taking off from the feet. Arms b), The left twist has been speeded by c) Half twist is complete. Arms in by
wide. Shoulders starting a little the cross-body throw of the right arm. chest. Body straight. Right shoulder
twist. Body straightening. moving forward into left twist.

Fig. 50. Rudolph (demonstrated by Ron Graham).

y

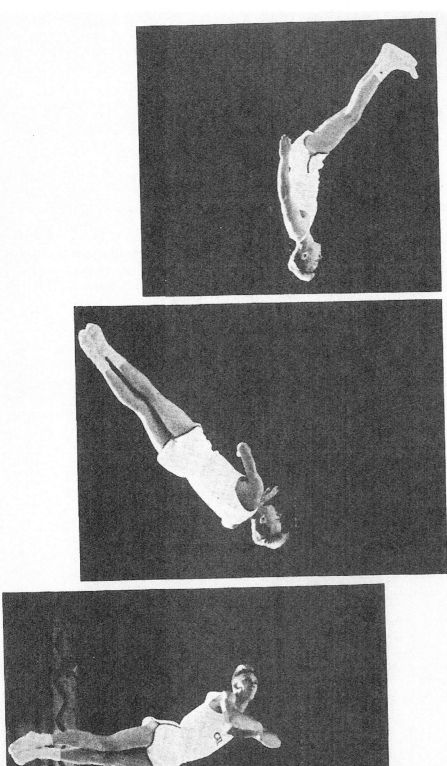

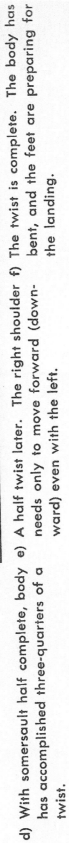

d) With somersault half complete, body e) A half twist later. The right shoulder f) The twist is complete. The body has
has accomplished three-quarters of a needs only to move forward (down- bent, and the feet are preparing for
twist. ward) even with the left. the landing.

Fig. 50. Continued.

our eyes on the bed as much of the time as possible, and avoid bending at the waist again until you see how much you need to bend to land on your feet.

B. Under-twisting is the other prevalent difficulty when trying to learn this stunt. As indicated before, the strong twist depends on getting a little start on the twist as you first bend over, having your arms wide at this time, throwing the arm across forcefully past the knees, pulling the arms in close to the body, and keeping the body straight while twisting.

C. Getting lost in the middle of the stunt and not knowing which way is up and which is down is due to not keeping the head in such a position as to see the bed almost the whole time. Developing this stunt from the barani and the barani-style full twisting forward somersaults and keeping the head in the right position during these stunts should help you to continue the same technique when adding the extra half twist necessary for the rudolph. If you do so, you will know where you are all of the time.

D. Those who learn the rudolph in the twisting belt without sufficient experience with the full twisting forward somersault often have trouble getting enough forward rotation. This is a result not so much of twisting too early as of twisting without having already started a strong forward somersault. To correct, postpone the twist and think first of forward bend; then twist.

ADDITIONAL TWISTING SOMERSAULTS LISTED:

1. Half twisting one-and-one-quarter forward somersault to sit landing (or back landing)

2. Half twisting one-and-one-quarter backward somersault to front landing

3. Half twisting three-quarters backward somersault to sit landing

4. Three-quarters barani to front landing

5. Full twisting three-quarters forward somersault to sit landing

6. Full twisting half-back somersault to front landing

7. Full twisting one-and-one-quarter backward somersault to sit or back landing

8. One-and-one-half twisting three-quarters forward somersault to front landing

9. One-and-one-half twisting backward somersault to feet

10. Double twisting backward somersault

9

Always More to Learn

One of the most intriguing things about trampolining is the almost endless variety of stunts and combinations of stunts that have been done or can be done on these bouncing beds. There is always another stunt ahead after the present one has been learned. There is almost always a way to improve your technique or form on the stunts you have already learned. There is the challenge of learning to do several repetitions of the same stunt in immediate succession and the even-greater challenge of doing a number of different stunts without any intermediate bounces in between.

The field of competitive trampolining offers many opportunities for new interest and new enthusiasm. The land of multiple somersaults and the fliffis invites the most daring to new adventures. Trampoline games are an almost unexplored field. Using the trampoline as a training device for competitive divers is a practice that has had some success and promises to have more. The neighborhood trampoline center is an institution with an interesting future and the backyard pit trampoline may outdo the backyard swimming pool before too many years. All in all, the immensity of the trampolining potential is a little overwhelming. Even though this book makes no pretense at "covering the field," it does seem appropriate to comment briefly on some of these many facets of the sport.

COMPETITIVE TRAMPOLINING

The history of high-level competition on the trampoline has followed a varied path. The early meets featured a few single stunts interspersed with a great deal of extra bouncing within a set time-limit on the trampoline. The trend from here was to feature a long, swing-time routine (one with no extra bounces between stunts), continuing for the entire time limit and leaving the trampolinist dizzy and exhausted. The time limit was shortened by the rules committee to lessen the hazard. The routines became more difficult and less controlled. The rules were changed again to provide for three eight-stunt, swing sequences with rest stops between, and more emphasis was put on form and control and less on daring difficulty. The three routines gave way to two and the two seem destined to be replaced by one of slightly longer, but still very limited, duration. Trampoline competition rules will probably be stabilized on a basis very similar to the competition in other gymnastic events; i.e., one consecutive routine of approximately ten stunts, and this routine will be judged a little more on the basis of form, control, continuity, beauty, style and freedom from errors and a little less on daring and difficulty.

MULTIPLE SOMERSAULTS, MULTIPLE TWISTERS, AND THE FLIFFIS

The top competitors on the trampoline and those with championship ambitions are doing stunts that you can't believe until you see them. They have only been hinted at previously in this book. The double somersaults (turning over twice before coming down), both forward and backward, have become commonplace. Triple somersaults are being done and will soon show up in competitive routines. The problem is to swing out of them or into them without any extra bounces so that they can be used in routines. Double twisting somersaults, two-and-a-half twisting somersaults, and triple twisters are an almost necessary part of a champion's routine. Three-and-a-half twisters and even quadruple twisters are not unknown in the practice sessions, but have not made their appearance in competition as yet.

The cody is another stunt that is coming of age. Double codys, full twisting codys, and even double twisting codys are currently routine competitive material. Various forms of the cody fliffis are being developed for future competitive use.

The term fliffis brings us to another fabulous field of stunts. These are the twisting double somersaults. The easiest fliffis is probably the double forward somersault with a half twist or barani in the second somersault. This is commonly called the barani-out fliffis. There is another fliffis which has the barani in the first somersault, so that the second somersault is a backward one. This is the barani-in fliffis. There is the back fliffis with a half twist in the second somersault and another with the half twist in the first somersault. There are some with full twists all in one somersault and no twist in the other and some with half twists in each of the two somersaults. The rudolph-out fliffis and the rudolph-in fliffis, the double twisting back fliffis, and the twisting triple somersault (triffie) are the ones currently challenging the top performers. There are many varieties that have not been seen in competition yet, and some that have only been done in someone's imagination. It is amazing to see what the human body can be trained to do. I hope that you someday will have an opportunity to see some of these wonderful stunts done by a champion.

USING THE TRAMPOLINE FOR TRAINING DIVERS

Springboard diving as a sport is at the present time a more widespread and better recognized event than trampolining. For one thing, it is a recognized international event, included in the Olympic Games competition. Trampolining does not seem destined to enjoy that distinction in the near future. The trampoline, however, has been useful and probably will be more so in the future as a means of improving the acrobatic ability of the top competitive divers. It can serve a similar but more modest purpose for you, too. You may be surprised and pleased at what a figure you can cut in the air over the swimming pool after you have had a few months of trampoline experience. Conversely you may find that some stunts that you want to learn on the trampoline can be more safely and fearlessly tried over the water from a springboard and transferred to the trampoline when the mechanics and confidence have been improved.

Some of the values which the trampoline has for training divers are fairly obvious. Because the trampoline is a dry and a warm place to practice, the workouts can be longer, and therefore the acquisition of more skill can take place as well as better conditioning. Because in trampoline practice it is not necessary to swim to the bank, climb out of the tank, and climb up to the board again as it is in diving, trampoline workouts can be more concentrated and the diver gets more done in the same length of time than he would practicing from the springboard. The use of the safety belt and the twisting safety belt for learning new acrobatic maneuvers and correcting faults is much more satisfactory over a trampoline than over the water.

There are, of course, limitations to the usefulness of the trampoline for training divers. The amount of rotation on somersaults is different for a good landing on the trampoline than it is for a good entry into the water. The diver's head-first entries obviously cannot be practiced on the trampoline except as duckunders to the back landing. The turned-up feet for landing on the trampoline can get to be a habit that makes the diver's feet-first entries into the water look as though he's wearing water skis. It is also true that the diver can get injuries on the trampoline which can hamper his diving progress. This can happen as a result of the diver not being adequately skilled in trampoline fundamentals before trying advanced stunts. Finally the diver needs to learn his acrobatics from the approach and hurdle or the standing start (for back-facing dives), neither of which are very practical on the trampoline. Also he needs many, many hours of practice on his springboard fundamentals to perfect his diving. This board practice must not be neglected in favor of trampoline bouncing. In summary, it is safe to say that practice on springboard diving and on trampolining can be of mutual assistance to each other when the individual's level of skill is fairly high on each, when the fundamentals of each are given full attention, and when the majority of practice time is put on the one in which the athlete intends to specialize. It is very rare, but not unknown, for the same person to be a champion in both events.

TRAMPOLINE GAMES

Informal fun on the trampoline for groups can often be enhanced by devising games which can be played with safety by performers of different levels of experience and ability.

One such game is called Move-Up. It is a follow-the-leader game with a judge-referee (usually the teacher) who decides who has done the stunt better than another. After the leader or the teacher names or demonstrates the stunt, each person in succession takes two tries at the stunt doing it in the best form he is able. If the judge thinks the person has done it better than the person ahead of him, he tells him to "move up one" in the line. He only considers the better of the performer's two attempts. If there are several people in line ahead of the person who has just performed and the judge feels that he has surpassed several of them, he can be moved up two or three places or even clear up to the head of the line. The one at the head of the line cannot move up, but, of course, he can be moved ahead of and thereby lose his place as leader. The line can surround the trampoline and rotate around as each one takes his turn. This is a good game to put the emphasis on form.

Another game is called Add-a-Stunt. This is also a sort of follow-the-leader game, but a bit more complicated. There are a number of variations, but this is one that has proved satisfactory. The first person does a stunt of his own choosing. The second person must do the same stunt and then add a stunt of his own. The third person must do both of the preceding stunts and then add one of his own choosing. That is as long as the sequence of stunts can become because the fourth person drops the first stunt and starts out by copying the two which have preceded him and adding his own. There is no rule against using the same stunt someone else has used. Whenever someone either fails to do the stunt he is copying or fails to do the stunt he is trying to add, he earns a "horse." When he gets three "horses" he is eliminated from the game. The next person after the one who has gotten a "horse" starts a new series. The stunts do not have to be in the same style or excellently done to get by, but have to be substantially complete. A referee is needed to make the game run smoothly.

Several additional specifications are necessary. The length of a stunt has to be limited in some way. One way is to rule that a maximum of two landings other than feet landings may intervene between the beginning and end of the stunt and that each stunt must begin and end on the feet. Thus a back drop to front drop to feet would qualify as one stunt. But a sit drop to a swivel hips to a barrel roll to feet would involve three landings between the take-off from the feet and the finish on the feet again and so would not qualify as a single stunt. Anyone using such an over-long stunt would get a "horse" charged to him.

The new stunt can be added to the previous one in either of two ways at the choice of the one adding it. It can be added in swing time (without any intervening bounces), in which case it must thereafter be copied in swing time; or it may be added with one or more extra bounces, in which case it can be copied with any number of extra bounces that the copier wishes to use. In adding a stunt in swing time, it is important to remember that the preceding stunt must be finished to the feet and that this landing is also the take-off into the new stunt that is being added.

It is usually necessary to control the difficulty of stunts which can be used in order to safeguard the least experienced or least skillful in the group. This can be done by limiting the stunts which can be used to a certain list or by outlawing certain stunts or groups of stunts, such as backward somersaults and twisting somersaults. After the game becomes familiar to the group, it is fun to play it without any verbal reminders so that each one has to remember what he is to do, or earn a penalty.

There are undoubtedly other equally good games that have been or can be originated. In fact, it is always safe to say that on the trampoline there are more games to be learned, more stunts to be mastered, more uses to be found, more complicated gyrations to be created, better ways of teaching to be discovered-in short, always more to learn!

Hand Balancing and Acrobatics Training for the Everyday Man and Woman

Prof. Paulinetti in a One Arm Planche

Bob Jones does His Famous 'Thumbs' Stand On Top of Indian Clubs

- Free Articles and Videos
- Classic Books
- DVD's and Courses
- Training Tools
- And More

Discover the Basics of Handstands and Tumbling to Super Advanced Stunts only at:

www.LostArtOfHandBalancing.com

Printed in Great Britain
by Amazon